TRUE TALES ꓴDOR YORK

Tony Morgan

Best Wishes

Tony

The Author

Tony Morgan lives near York in the North of England.

- *True Tales of Tudor York* is Tony's second non-fiction history book.

- *Power, Treason and Plot in Tudor England - Margaret Clitherow an Elizabethan Saint* is Tony's first non-fiction book. Published by Pen and Sword Books in 2022, it explores the religious power struggles of Tudor England, their impact on York and the tragic life and death of Margaret Clitherow.

- *The Pearl of York, Treason and Plot* is Tony's most recent novel. Set in the dark streets of Tudor York, the book tells the tragic story of Margaret Clitherow through the eyes of a youthful Guy Fawkes.

- *7th November 1617* explores what may have happened if the Gunpowder Plot had succeeded.

- *Remember, Remember the 6th of November* is Tony's first novel, a taut thriller set in the final days of the Gunpowder Plot.

The profits from Tony's books and history talks have raised thousands of pounds for **St Leonard's Hospice** in York.

https://tonymorganauthor.wordpress.com/

Foreword

Dear reader,

This book is about the history of York during the reign of the Tudors, the people who lived there and those who shaped their lives. The whole Tudor dynasty is covered from the incidents which up led to the coronation of Henry VII in 1485 to slightly after the death of Elizabeth I in 1603. The subject matter focuses on the events of the period, aspects of life in the city and the people who lived there.

The contents include royal visits, rebellions, religious unrest, plagues, earthquakes, flooding, the treatment of the poor and ordinary life. If you've ever been to York, you'll recognise many of the streets and buildings as they still exist today. If you haven't, I don't work for the tourist board, but I do hope the book inspires you to pay a visit to this wonderful history-filled place.

If you already live in York or Yorkshire, or have relatives from the area, you might recognise some familiar names. People sometimes mention to me that I name-dropped one of their ancestors during my history talks.

For ease of reading, the years examined in the book use the current Gregorian calendar format. Each year is considered to begin on 1 January, rather than on 25 March. I've also used modern spellings when using quotations from contemporary Tudor records. In historical documents the names of people and places are often spelled in many different ways. I've opted to use a single standard spelling where feasible. If you carry out your own research and reading, you may find some slight variations in the names and years depending on the sources you use.

When I set out to write the book, my objectives were primarily to *inform* and *entertain*. As such, I've taken a decision not to include footnotes and citations and so on. If you plan to do your own research, I trust you'll find the bibliography at the back of the book useful.

I'm deeply indebted to many people down the centuries who have documented events, practices and the lives of people who lived in York, maintained such records, or meticulously researched them. Without each of these groups, this book wouldn't be possible. Thank you.

Finally, I'd like to dedicate this book to the many people who organise and attend local history societies and similar groups. Organisers - you work so hard and ask for nothing in return. Members - you brave the weather, listen intently and ask great questions. I appreciate you all.

Yours sincerely,

Tony Morgan.

Map of Late Tudor York

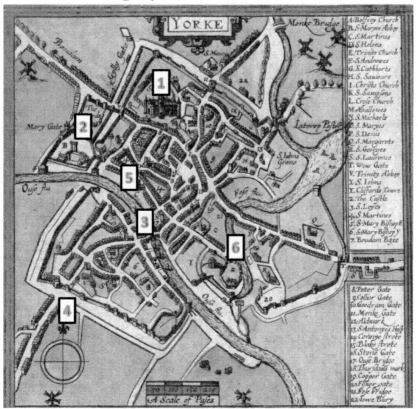

The map above was created by the renowned Tudor cartographer John Speed at the very beginning of the Stuart era. As this was after the Dissolution, most of York's religious houses were closed by this time.

1. York Minster
2. Site of St Mary's Abbey and the King's Manor (office of the Council of the North)
3. Ouse Bridge (the only crossing in York over the Ouse)
4. Micklegate Bar (main route into York from London)
5. Common Hall (Guildhall, office of Corporation of York)
6. York Castle (including Tudor York's main prison)

Introduction

In the first century AD the Romans built a fortress on the banks of the river Ouse, near to where the smaller river Foss flows into it. The Romans named their settlement E*boracum*. To the Anglo-Saxons it was *Eoforwic*, while the Vikings called the place *Jorvik*. The village, town and city which eventually grew there, and today is known as York, is steeped in history. At least partially, this is due to its strategic location. As the centuries went by, the place became a natural crossroads. This brought together the main north-south route which linked London and Scotland and a more local east-west connection between the Ridings of Yorkshire and the port of Hull, with the North Sea and Europe beyond.

Not long after 1066, the Normans arrived. In order to gain control of the area, they built a castle. This was soon destroyed, and its garrison killed in an uprising which was widely supported by the Danes, Anglo-Saxons and local people. William the Conqueror's response was devastating, the so-called *"Harrying of the North"*. During the following centuries, new and improved fortifications were built. The city's walls were reconstructed in stone, building upon and replacing the previous banks of earth and wooden ramparts. York became home to a growing number of religious houses. Trade and prosperity came to the city.

King Edward I established York as the centre of his operations for seemingly endless wars with the Scots. For several years around 1300, the city became a de facto capital of England. A century later in 1396, King Richard II granted York its royal charter. This accorded the city the same status as if it was a county in its own right and freed it from the jurisdiction of the wider Yorkshire. With York's leaders directly responsible to the crown, their loyalty was expected. At times during the Tudor period this relationship was severely strained, and its limits tested.

Under the charter, the city was administered by a tiered body working under the legal name of the Corporation of York. The Corporation's leaders created a system and a structure for local government which continued without significant change in the city until the nineteenth century.

Long before that, during the fourteenth and first half of the fifteenth century York was a city on the up, a place buoyed by the wealth of its religious houses, textile-related crafts and position as the region's administrative capital. Its growing prosperity resulted in a rising population. This is believed to have peaked at around fifteen or sixteen thousand people. Although this may not be huge when compared to the modern day (the 2021 census estimates the district population as being over two hundred thousand), York was the second most populous city in the whole of England, only behind London. To all intents and purposes, York was the capital of the North and the second city of the land.

As we know, these things come and go in cycles. By the time of the Tudors in the closing stages of the fifteenth century, the population was already in decline. It continued to fall until the reign of Elizabeth I. An examination of the reasons behind this drastic change in circumstance uncovers some disturbing parallels with modern times. The city was suffering from a combination of structural economic change, unrest and bouts of pestilence.

Yorkshire's economic landscape as a whole was changing. For centuries, wool production and cloth-making had been dominant major industries across most of Medieval England.

This was still the case during the second half of the fifteenth century. However, the local epicentre for the trade had moved westwards across the Ridings of Yorkshire. Traditional locations such as York were being displaced as wool processing centres by the expanding towns of the West Riding including Halifax and Leeds. Where the money went, people soon followed.

A second major cause for York's population decline was disease. Before and during the reign of the Tudors, a number of widespread epidemics, including bubonic plague, smallpox, sweating sickness and new strains of influenza, swept across the British Isles. With their citizens often cramped together in close proximity and with poor sanitary conditions, England's more urban locations were often inordinately affected.

York was no exception. As we'll see, up until the reign of Elizabeth I the city's population was impacted by continuing outbreaks of disease. There were indirect impacts too. Many people became more wary of living in urban conurbations. For a time, immigration from the surrounding areas and from further afield was much reduced.

The next few lines may sound familiar. In the time before and later on during the reign of the Tudors, England's relationship with mainland Europe and Scotland might best be described as strained. The country's leaders and population were often divided. These issues led to unrest, outbreaks of rebellion and war. Each had an impact on York's population. Men from York served their country and died during the Hundred Years War, for example, against the French. When this finally ended (almost) in 1453, England withdrew from Europe and quickly turned its attentions and frustrations in on itself.

The Wars of the Roses raged on for three decades. A number of major battles took place in Yorkshire. Once again men from York were killed during the combat. This time they died fighting on both sides of the divide. Some fought for the

"Yorkists" and others for the *"Lancastrians"*. As many readers will know, this wasn't a clash between the two northern cities, but betwixt two competing sections of the Plantagenet dynasty. Each of the House of York and the House of Lancaster had a competing claim for the English throne.

This book is about Tudor York rather than the Wars of the Roses, but it's worth completing this introduction with some background to cover the later stages of the conflict. In particular, of course, we'll focus on its relevance to York. If you're not interested in this, or know a lot about it already, of course feel free to skip onto the next section.

In December 1460, Richard Duke of York, was killed by Lancastrian forces loyal to King Henry VI at the Battle of Wakefield. His defeat (probably) gave rise to the mnemonic *"Richard of York Gave Battle In Vain"*, which reminds us of the order of the colours of the rainbow. More importantly, although Richard's body was buried at Pontefract, his head was brought to York where it was displayed on a spike above Micklegate Bar wearing nothing but a paper crown.

Three months later in March 1461, Richard's son and heir Edward was proclaimed as King Edward IV of England. His army had been victorious against the Lancastrians at the deadly and decisive Battle of Towton, just a dozen miles southwest of York. Towton is adjudged to have been the bloodiest battle ever fought on the British mainland. Estimates of the dead vary widely. Some start at around three thousand men. Others go as high as twenty-eight thousand. Either way, it was a lot of people to lose, and many more people were injured or maimed.

Afterwards Edward marched on to York where it is thought the Lancastrians may have set up a temporary government. As the new King's army arrived in the city, the previous monarch Henry VI and his wife Queen Margaret managed to escape. Eventually they were forced into exile in Europe.

Naturally, Edward issued orders for his father's head be taken down. It was replaced by the severed head of an executed Lancastrian leader. Sometime later after Easter, Edward marched south and prepared for his formal coronation.

King Edward IV was to return to York two more times over the next two years, in both 1462 and 1463. While the King was there, he made payments to the city's people and thanked them for their support for his armies during recent military campaigns in Scotland and the Borders.

In 1470, events took another turn. Henry VI returned from his exile and seized the throne. This time it was Edward who was forced to flee across the English Channel to the continent, but he didn't remain there for long. He soon returned to England with a plan to retake his kingdom. Edward landed with a small army at Ravenspurn on the east coast of Yorkshire, not too far from Hull. The site can no longer be visited, as it's been lost over the years due to coastal erosion.

Edward travelled with his men inland from the coast first to Beverley, before marching on towards York. When he reached the city walls, he and his army were refused entry. It was only after Edward confirmed to the city's leaders that he'd returned to England to reclaim the duchy of York, rather than take back the crown, that he was permitted inside. The gates swung open, and Edward and his representatives entered York through Walmgate Bar.

"Furnished with money from the citizens", he was soon on his way again. Edward marched south with his force towards London. Soon afterwards and despite his promises in York, he reclaimed the crown and had Henry VI imprisoned. After his own son and heir was killed in a subsequent battle, Henry also died. He was very probably murdered under Edward's orders.

With his main rivals now dead, Edward recognised the importance of the north, or perhaps its capacity for rebellion. He stripped many of the prime northern estates from the Lancastrian leaders and granted the lands and castles to his brother Richard, the Duke of Gloucester. Amongst Richard's new properties were castles at Middleham and Sheriff Hutton, the latter being only about ten miles away from York.

Around the same time, King Edward established the Council of the North, with his brother Richard as its first Lord President and its headquarters located in Richard's castle at Sheriff Hutton. If Edward's vision had been to create a royal body to oversee and improve matters across the counties of Northern England, including in York and in Yorkshire, we might consider this be an early version of regional devolution or even (and forgive me for using the phrase) *"levelling up"*. Primarily though it acted as a court of law.

In subsequent years, Richard spent a great deal of his time in and around York. Even more than that, he began to make arrangements for his body to eventually be buried there. The plans included the creation of a grand tomb in a chantry chapel attached to York Minster. As we now know, these plans came to nought.

When Edward IV died of natural causes in April 1483, he was succeeded by his twelve-year-old son, who became King Edward V. As the boy's uncle, Richard was named his Lord Protector of the Realm. Richard travelled to York, held a service of remembrance for his brother in the Minster and pledged his loyalty and allegiance to the new young King.

However, claims had been made that Edward IV's marriage had not been legally valid. The implication of this was that the new King and his brother had both been born illegitimately and so had no rightful claim to the throne. After a statute was signed invalidating the marriage, the Lord Protector was crowned King Richard III in July 1483. The two princes were placed in the Tower of London and never seen of again. Of course, there's more to the story than that, but this is a book about the Tudor period, so we're going to skip over it.

Following his coronation in Westminster Abbey, King Richard travelled to York for a second coronation. The city records state:

"King Richard the Third, with his Queen and son, came to York, where they were received with great honour, and crowned for the second time by Archbishop Rotherham in the Minster, and his son invested in the Principality of Wales. For joy whereof there were stage plays, tournaments and other triumphant sports. The King knighting his base {illegitimate} son Richard of Gloucester, and many other gentlemen of these parts."

The new King remained in York for three long celebratory weeks. Despite constant claims of their poverty, York's leaders must have had to invest heavily in the festivities. There were good reasons for them to do this. With Richard feeling such goodwill towards the city, it was a great time to ask him for some favours. The Corporation of York's leaders requested and gained tentative promises to reduce the fee farm, the annual tax the city was forced to collect to pay to the crown and the nobility. The hope was to relieve some of the economic pressure being felt by the city's residents and leaders.

Richard also had to consider how best to govern the whole of the north of his new kingdom, including how to continue to operate the Council of the North. With his own hands full administering the rest of the country, Richard appointed his nephew John de la Pole, the Earl of Lincoln, as the new Lord President.

Shortly afterwards, the Wars of the Roses broke out once more when in 1485 Henry Tudor, who had been in exile in France, assembled an army of English, Welsh, Scottish and French troops. After a great deal of political posturing, manoeuvring and changing of sides, Henry's army eventually defeated King Richard's own forces at the Battle of Bosworth Field in Leicestershire.

Richard was to be the last King of England (at least to date) to die in battle, but there was to be no grand state funeral in Westminster Abbey, or a magnificent chantry built for him in York. Instead, Richard's battered remains were dumped unceremoniously into the ground and interred in an unmarked grave in the East Midlands. There they remained until the discovery of his skeleton beneath a car park in Leicester in 2012.

Richard's death in 1485 was the end of the Plantagenet era. Henry Tudor declared himself, by right of conquest, to be the rightful King of England. One of the first laws made during Henry VII's first Parliament was to repeal the statute which had invalidated the marriage of Edward IV.

This was important because Henry was married to King Edward's daughter, Elizabeth of York. Clearly, one of the objectives of this marriage had been to unite the Houses of York and Lancaster. The idea was by doing so it would put an end to the dispute between the two Houses for once and for all and, more importantly for Henry, would secure his place on the throne.

With the Wars of the Roses seemingly over, the Tudor era could now begin…

CHAPTER ONE
The Corporation of York

We're now ready to begin our examination proper of the history, events and the people of York during the Tudor period. We'll begin with the reign of Henry VII. Before we do so, it's worth taking a quick look at the structure of the Corporation of York. A high-level understanding of this is going to be a very useful companion for the remainder of the book.

With the pre-Tudor introduction and preamble complete, if you're chomping at the bit to find out what went on in Tudor York, I understand a few readers might wish to skip this chapter. Whether you do or you don't, you still might want to pop back now and then to gain a better understanding for example of how some of the men mentioned could progress on to become a sheriff, an alderman or even Lord Mayor.

The leader of the Corporation of York was the city's mayor. By Tudor times the mayor had been bestowed with the somewhat grander title of Lord Mayor, as in London. The Lord Mayor of York worked closely with his twelve fellow aldermen. When Richard II granted York the city its royal charter in 1396, the King presented the city's mayor with a ceremonial sword. By tradition, the blade of this sword should always be pointed upwards, apart from when in the presence of the monarch.

The thirteen aldermen were responsible for the most important decisions taken in York. They were also the city's leading justices of the peace, presiding over many of the higher profile court hearings in the city. As well as standard criminal courts, the Corporation operated specialist courts of law on subjects such as deeds and wills, apprenticeships and the treatment of orphans. In addition, separate courts were adjudicated by the Council of the North, the Church and a travelling assizes court. York was obviously a good place to be for lawyers and other legal officials.

The Corporation's responsibilities included maintaining local laws, raising taxes, ensuring people adhered to non-religious and sometimes religious policies and much else besides. The aldermen were supported by an additional council known as the Twenty-Four. While the number of aldermen was fixed at thirteen men (in Tudor times there was only men) which included the Lord Mayor, the number of members of the Twenty-Four ebbed up and down over time.

Beneath the Twenty-Four was another body called the Common Council. Prior to 1517, the Common Council was also known as the Forty-Eight. The Common Council played a much more minor role in the city's administration. However, it did provide a voice for some of the more junior freemen in the city and, for some, a route towards the higher echelons of York's local government.

The Corporation paid for York's two Members of Parliament and employed many other men to undertake a variety of roles. The city employed an official recorder, a common clerk and a keeper of weights and measures. In addition, there were many support jobs for cooks, prison wardens, masons and so on.

The mayor's office included additional paid staff, such the mayor's sword bearer, the mace bearer and sergeants. The mayor was also supported in his duties by the two Sheriffs of York. Each sheriff had their own staff, with additional men responsible for making arrests and so on.

As you can see, the Corporation was a sizeable organisation, but how did a man in York get onto the

Corporation ladder and what sort of men were they? At this stage, it's important to note that the Corporation wasn't an organisation led by the local nobility. Most of the men who joined the Twenty-Four or became aldermen were different. These were mainly men of business, merchants who bought and sold goods, skilled tradesmen, craftsmen and such like. We'll examine the activities of a number of these men in the coming chapters.

One of the pre-requisites for the majority of would-be Corporation office holders was that they first had to be made a freeman of the city. Freedom of the City of York conferred on its holders special rights to trade in York. Usually this was as a member of the one of the city's official trade guilds.

Traditionally, there were three ways a man could become a freeman in York. The first was by birth. This right could be inherited by someone who learned from and followed the same trade as their father. The second route towards becoming a freeman was by serving an official apprenticeship in a recognised trade or guild. The third approach was perhaps the more modern way. Some men, particularly *"immigrants"* who had arrived in the city from outside York could be allowed, at an agreed price, to purchase their freedom.

Freedom didn't just give an opportunity to hold office. It allowed men to vote in certain local elections and conferred them with wider rights and benefits in the city. For example, people who weren't freemen could only buy from or sell goods in York to people who were.

During the time of the Tudors, a small number of women also managed to gain freedom to trade in the city. Professor David Palliser's excellent research identifies that of more than six thousand people who gained the freedom of York between 1500 and 1603, only forty-four were female. Primarily these women achieved their freedom through inheritance. Mostly this was accomplished by a widow taking over the business of her dead husband. None of them, however, became an officer of the Corporation.

The very first step onto the corporate ladder for an ambitious freeman in York was to gain an appointment into one of several minor administrative roles, such as bridgemaster or muremaster. The bridgemasters were responsible for maintaining the city's bridges over the rivers Ouse and Foss, while the muremasters attended to the upkeep of the city's walls. These roles were held for a single year, at which time a different freeman would be elected to take over the position.

Typically, after serving as a bridgemaster or muremaster, the man might be invited to serve for a second year in office as one of the city's chamberlains. This role was an important one as it included managing elements of the city's finances. The chamberlains dealt with income and expenditures and acted as the city's treasurers.

Although many of these minor roles were unpaid, they were much sought after. As well as providing a route towards becoming a councillor, they provided future members of the Common Council, Twenty-Four and aldermen with valuable experience and insights into what it took to run the city.

Some of the wealthier freemen of York were sometimes able to skip the first step of serving as a bridgemaster or muremaster. They could do so by making a direct payment to the Corporation. If the payment was accepted, they'd be allowed to progress directly on to become one of the city's chamberlains. A very small number of men also gained direct entry to the Corporation at a higher level. Of the hundred and six men who served as an alderman in York during the sixteenth century, ninety-nine of them had earlier spent at least a year as a chamberlain.

Once a freeman had been a chamberlain, he would likely

progress on to become a member of the Common Council and take part in minor administrative duties. The next step beyond this was more significant. Each year, two men were elected to serve for an annual term (which began on 29 September) as one of the city's two sheriffs. When their term of office was complete, the sheriffs were almost always invited to join the Twenty-Four. They would then become involved in many of York's more important Corporation activities.

The next step after the Twenty-Four was to be elected as an alderman. This was a much tougher move to make. A man could only become an alderman when an existing incumbent alderman died, retired through ill-heath or, very rarely, was disenfranchised by his colleagues. Either way, the remaining eleven aldermen and the Lord Mayor would play a major role in the election of an appropriate member of the Twenty-Four to join their ranks.

Once a year on 15 January, the aldermen met to elect one of their own to serve for an annual term as the city's Lord Mayor. Unlike the sheriffs who commenced their own term in September, the mayor's year in office began on 3 February. Aldermen could serve as the Lord Mayor on multiple occasions, although once they'd held the office they would usually have to wait until their fellow aldermen had each had their own turn as mayor before they could take the role again.

The Lord Mayor of York wasn't a ceremonial role. The mayor was an important man. He set the Corporation agenda (sometimes in his own favour), gave the casting vote at major Corporation meetings, monitored and managed prices in York's markets and could even get people arrested. York's mayors reported directly to the King or Queen of England of the day, although most interactions went through members of the Privy Council or other supporting officials.

The Corporation was an organisation run by the city's

businessmen. More than seventy per cent of York's aldermen during the sixteenth century were merchants or wholesale traders. Another twenty-five per cent consisted of craftsmen and retailers. Of the rest, five per cent were gentlemen or lawyers.

The Twenty-Four, however, had a lesser concentration of merchants and a much wider set of trades and guilds were represented. Men in certain trades and crafts were probably well aware that the Twenty-Four would be as far as they could rise. For example, there were twelve butchers in the Twenty-Four in York during the sixteenth century but not one of them progressed on to the next step and became an alderman.

The main offices of the Corporation were located in a fine building constructed in the fifteenth century known as the Common Hall. This could be accessed by boat from the river Ouse or by horse drawn vehicle or on foot from Coney Street. Today the building is known as the Guildhall. The Corporation's successor, the City of York Council still hold some of their major meetings there.

If you ever find yourself walking down Coney Street in York, you can pop down the alley and have a look at the building. It was badly damaged during the Second World War but has since been restored. The fine stained-glass window which depicts scenes from York's long history was installed in 1960.

The Corporation also maintained and used other buildings in the city. For example, there were offices on Ouse Bridge, which were often used for Corporation meetings. There were also two prisons on or next to Ouse Bridge.

We'll explore a lot more about the Corporation of York, many of its office holders and what they got up to during the reign of the Tudors in the coming chapters. We'll also examine the Corporation's important and sometimes fractious relationship with the King's or Queen's Council of the North.

CHAPTER TWO
Henry VII - Part One

When Henry VII became the first Tudor King of England in August 1485, the city of York found itself to be in an awkward situation. The Corporation had previously been on very good terms with the former regime, particularly the final Plantagenet monarch Richard III. During the final days of Richard's reign, they'd even sent eighty men led by the city's mace bearer to fight for him at the Battle of Bosworth Field. Thankfully for all concerned, the men from York arrived too late to take part in the fighting.

When the Corporation heard of Richard's death, they wrote this angry statement:

"King Richard, late mercifully reigning upon us, was, through great treason of the Duke of Norfolk and many others that turned against him, with many other lords and nobles of the North, was piteously slain and murdered, to the great heaviness of this city."

Soon afterwards, Henry VII's envoy arrived in York to proclaim his master was the new King of England. The Corporation's officials arranged to meet the envoy inside the relative safety of the thick walls of York Castle, partly at least for the envoy's own protection.

During the first year of his reign, King Henry wanted to see changes made to the Corporation of York and attempted to appoint a number of his own supporters into some of the city's administrative positions. However, his nominations were rejected by the Corporation who instead employed their own preferred candidates. For example, following the death of the city's recorder Miles Metcalfe (a supporter of Richard III who'd held the position since 1477), the Corporation was placed under pressure to appoint Richard Green from the Earl of Northumberland's staff. In spite of this, they held out and eventually appointed a local man John Vavasour, who'd supported Richard III.

There must have been trepidation then a year later when the Corporation of York heard the new King of England was planning his first royal visit to the city in April 1486. The Corporation and York's population as a whole had two choices. They could give Henry and his entourage a frosty reception or they could welcome the King into their city with open arms and demonstrate their loyalty to the new Tudor regime. Tactfully, they chose the latter.

The Lord Mayor of York in 1486 was William Chimney. He dispatched the city's two sheriffs, John Beverley and Roger Appleby, two aldermen and a group of accompanying men to Tadcaster, where they welcomed the King at the site of an earlier version of the current bridge over the river Wharfe. A few miles closer to York in Bilbrough, the party was joined by Lord Mayor Chimney, himself, the city's other aldermen and several additional dignitaries. All were resplendent in their ceremonial robes.

The party proceeded on to York. At Dringhouses the city's population received their first sight of the King but the pageant was only just beginning. At the entrance to the city's walls at Micklegate Bar, a huge scene had been constructed which depicted a red and white rose as the symbol of Henry's bringing together of the Houses of York and Lancaster. As part of the very warm welcome into the city, a proclamation was read out to King Henry declaring he was being given *the city, key and crown to rule and redress"*.

As the party travelled on down the hill of Micklegate and across Ouse Bridge, Henry was met by actors who played out the roles of the six previous King Henrys. Their parts were followed by King Solomon who when he met the new King asked him to govern the land and the city *"righteously by politic providence"*. Once across the river Ouse, the parade entered Coney Street and made its way to the Corporation's offices at the Common Hall. Outside this building, Henry was presented with a *"sword of victory"* by King David. The procession and celebrations continued on through the centre of York towards York Minster. In the street of Stonegate, Henry was met by the Virgin Mary who committed to *"sue to my Son to send you His grace"*. The pageant and parties continued well into the night.

The Corporation spent £66 on King Henry's first visit to York. The Bank of England's inflation calculator estimates this to be equivalent to over £60,000 in November 2022 terms. This doesn't seem very much by modern standards, but this sort of comparison is notoriously difficult to make. We shouldn't forget how relatively little the price of labour and materials was back then compared with today, and the Corporation wouldn't have had to stump up for the huge policing and overtime costs. The King's army provided most of the security anyway.

The Corporation's leaders would certainly have been of the opinion they'd spent a great deal of money on the King's visit, perhaps almost as much or even more that they had on Richard III's second coronation a few years earlier. They must have hoped it was worth it. Clearly, they wanted to declare the city's loyalty to the new King.

Just as they'd done when Richard III had visited them, the aldermen pleaded the city's poverty to Henry, telling him that under the previous regime York had become *"prostrated, decayed and wasted"*. In addition, they reminded the King of the promises made by Richard to reduce the city's fee farm, York's annual tax payment to the Exchequer. For some time, the fee had been set at a flat rate of £160. To all intents and purposes, this was a tax on the city which had to be raised by the Corporation using income from tolls, rents, court fines and other taxes. Part of the £160 was paid to the crown, while other payments would be made to certain nobles and agents of the King.

The grand welcome and subsequent pleas offered by Lord Mayor Chimney and his colleagues must have impressed Henry. After his visit to York, the King agreed that a significant part of the city's fee farm payment could be waived. However, discussions regarding specific details, exact amounts and how this should be achieved rumbled on for some time.

Henry is reported as having shown some sympathy for the plight of York when he returned to London, *"At our last being at our city there, seeing the great ruin and extreme decay that the same is fallen in"*. The Corporation leaders must have issued a collective sigh of relief and hoped they wouldn't be forced to shell out again for a similar extravagant event any time soon.

CHAPTER THREE
Henry VII - Part Two

The most significant uprising during the early years of Henry VII's reign culminated in what is now considered to have been a brief resumption and the final battle of the Wars of the Roses. As always, the city of York had a part to play.

The man entrusted by Richard III to be his successor as Lord President of the Council of the North was his nephew John de la Pole, the Earl of Lincoln. After Richard's death, Lincoln made his peace with and promised his loyalty to Henry VII. Secretly though he retained an allegiance to the Yorkist cause.

Lincoln and other Yorkist supporters claimed a young man called Lambert Simnel was in fact Edward V, the older of the two princes who'd disappeared after being locked up in the Tower of London by Richard III. If his identify was true, then Henry VII had inadvertently given the boy a route to his own throne by revalidating King Edward IV's marriage.

A number of Yorkists rallied to the call. Lincoln and his allies formed an army and began a new rebellion against Henry VII. In June 1487, they defeated a smaller Lancastrian force during a minor skirmish on Bramham Moor near to Tadcaster. Following their victory, the rebels' confidence grew. However, a much larger army, who were loyal to King Henry VII and led by one of his supporters Henry Percy, the Earl of Northumberland, had been sent to confront them.

Facing the oncoming challenge, a section of the Yorkist forces led by Lord Scrope broke off from the main group and headed off towards York. When they arrived at the city, they attempted to break through the city's walls via the gates at Bootham Bar.

If the rebels proved to be successful in getting inside and taking control of the city, they'd be able to use York as a fortified base for the rebellion. How would York's citizens react? Not so long ago, their city had been loyal to Richard III of the House of York. More recently though they'd welcomed and pledged their allegiance to the new Tudor king Henry VII.

It appears not everyone in the city embraced the warm welcome the Corporation had given to Henry Tudor. During the melee, one of York's senior aldermen William Wells was killed. It's believed he was murdered by one of his own citizens. Was this evidence of York's mixed and perhaps wavering loyalty?

Before his death, Wells had followed the standard route towards the top of the Corporation. In 1467, he'd been elected as one of the two Sheriffs of York. After this, he'd joined the Twenty-Four and eventually been made an alderman. Eight years before his death, in 1479 he'd served as the Lord Mayor of York. His family lived in the parish of St Michael Le Belfrey next to York Minster. He'd obviously not been expecting to be killed. At the time of his death, Alderman Wells hadn't yet written a will. In the following months the *"administration of his goods was granted to Alice his widow"*.

Lord Scrope's men led a fierce attack on the city walls. The gates at Bootham Bar were stoutly defended by Corporation officials supported by York citizens who'd remained loyal to the crown. Following Alderman Wells' death, the Lord Mayor William Todd personally orchestrated the city's defence. He was supported in this task by another alderman Richard York.

When their assault was finally rebuffed, Lord Scrope and his men headed north. They were soon to be followed by the Earl of Northumberland's army. The rebels' leader, the Earl of

Lincoln, seized this opportunity to avoid the King's approaching force.

The main Yorkist group under Lincoln now moved south. Eventually, they were confronted by a larger army headed by Henry VII, himself. Battle lines were drawn up at Stoke Field near Newark. The ensuing engagement is considered by many to be the final battle of the Wars of the Roses. The Yorkist forces were routed. Many of the defeated army's leaders, including the Earl of Lincoln, were killed during the battle or executed afterwards.

The would-be pretender to the throne, Lambert Simnel, was arrested. Although he was declared to be an imposter, surprisingly Simnel wasn't executed. Instead, Henry spared his life and forgave him. Simnel was pardoned and allowed to earn a living in a menial job in the royal family kitchens. Lord Scrope, the man who'd led the attack on York, was also spared execution. He was fined and ordered to remain in London where a close watch was placed upon him.

In July 1487, not long after the battle of Stoke Field, Henry VII marched his army towards York. This time the city had received little notice of the royal visit. There was insufficient time to be able to prepare for an elaborate celebration with actors, displays and pageantry in the city's streets. When the King arrived in York, he quickly sought out William Todd and Richard York. He knighted them both for their bravery in leading the city's defence against Lord Scrope's attack and for their loyalty to the crown. The pair were also given annual pensions.

Following the sobering execution of a number of the rebels, it was time to party once again in York. The Corporation quickly organised for a performance to be held of the city's Corpus Christi plays in front of the King. During the impromptu celebrations which followed, the city was reported to have been *"drunken dry"*. We must assume the Corporation sent out men with wagons or carts to the neighbouring towns and villages to top up supplies. It wouldn't be the done thing to keep the King and his men thirsty.

Not long after King Henry left York, there was a second celebration in the city. In a show of his personal thanks for the city's loyalty, the Earl of Northumberland had made a large donation of venison to the Corporation. This was put to good use in September 1487 when a great feast was held in the Common Hall. The Lord Mayor, aldermen, many councillors and other York citizens sat down together to eat a grand banquet, washed down with *"red wine sufficient without anyone paying for the same"*. It appears the supplies of alcohol had already been replenished.

In 1587, the Lord Mayor of York William Todd was a busy man. In addition to leading the defence of the city, gaining his knighthood and organising for plays and celebrations to be held for the King, he is reported to have organised much needed repairs to sixty yards of the city's walls at Fishergate at his own expense. If you visit Fishergate Bar today, you will see a plaque commemorating his work which proclaims: *"A doi m.cccclxxx vii Sr Willm Tod knight mayre this wal was mayd in his days lx yadys"*.

Like many of York's aldermen, Willian Todd was a merchant. When he died in 1502 *"he gave his body to be buried in Our Ladies Quire within the Church of All Hallows in the Pavement"*. The church is known today as All Saint's Church.

Just two years after he'd paid for the Fishergate walls to be repaired, Todd must have been sorely disappointed. The city walls of York were about to come under attack once again.

CHAPTER FOUR
Henry VII - Part Three

Despite the generous gift of a great deal of venison to the city of York, the Earl of Northumberland wasn't a popular man with everyone in Yorkshire. Before the Battle of Bosworth Field, he'd acted on the side of Richard III. However, when he arrived at Bosworth, he'd opted not to lead his forces into the battle. Many Yorkists and some historians believe this decision played a crucial role in Richard's defeat. After he was initially held in custody, Northumberland was released by Henry VII and the Earl swore his allegiance to the new King. For those who remained loyal to Richard III and the House of York, Northumberland's actions could only be viewed as those of a traitor.

In 1489, Northumberland was travelling around Yorkshire levying taxes. This included raising an unpopular new tax recently approved by Parliament to fund a new war for the King in Brittany. It was a time of unrest in Yorkshire with rumours of rebellion. When the Earl visited a location near Thirsk, he was surrounded by an angry mob and killed. Whether the motive for his murder was rage against the tax, vengeance for Richard III or a bit of both remains unclear.

News of the Earl's death spread quickly through Yorkshire and a popular uprising soon began. Unlike many of the other rebellions, this one wasn't led by members of the nobility. Instead, it was initiated and led primarily by local craftsmen and yeomen. Gatherings to organise the men and their actions were held at Allerton Moor near Leeds, Gatherley Moor near Richmond and outside Sheriff Hutton.

For a time, York found itself once again the centre of attention for a new group of rebels. Hearing of the attack on the Earl of Northumberland, the Lord Mayor and aldermen began to set up defences in the city. They also sent *"three sharp men... into the country... to understand the demeanour of the commons"*. In addition, word was sent to the King about the uprising and that the city might soon need his support in order to defend itself.

In May 1489, the rebels attacked York. During the fighting and chaos which ensued, Walmgate Bar was burned down and Fishergate Bar badly damaged. Sir William Todd must have looked at his purse and wondered if he'd be forced to shell out once again to pay for more repairs to the city walls. There's no record that he ever did though.

Critically for the rebels, they were supported by a number of sympathisers who were positioned within York itself, including at least one of the city's aldermen, Thomas Wrangwyshe. With the help of those inside, the attackers gained access to the centre of the city by breaking through the damaged entry gates of Walmgate and Fishergate Bar.

Once inside the city, the rebels beseeched the Corporation's leaders to throw York's support behind the new uprising. Thankfully for the Corporation, even before King Henry had had time to march an army north, the rebels had left York and the rebellion had started to peter out.

The Lord Mayor and the aldermen denied they'd ever considered supporting or felt any sympathy at all for the rebels, and the city managed to escape without major punishment. This could not be said, however, for many of the rebels' leaders. On his way to York, the King ordered for trials and executions to take place in Pontefract, at Ferrybridge and in Wentbridge.

When news reached the Corporation that King Henry was heading towards their city once more, Alderman Wrangwyshe was arrested. Sir William Todd and Sir Richard York, who had led York's previous defence and been knighted by the King, were dressed up in their finest livery, placed on horses and sent out of the city along with twelve sergeants to meet the King and his army en route.

Henry VII was greeted by the aldermen once more in Tadcaster, before finding comfortable lodgings for himself in the official residence of the Archbishop of York at the Bishop's Palace in Bishopthorpe just a few miles outside of York.

In the coming days, a number of the rebels were tried in the Common Hall, found guilty of treason and sentenced to death. Alderman Wrangwyshe was one of those found guilty. In his case it was due to his role in enabling the rebels to enter York.

John Chambers of Ayton was found guilty of the murder of the Earl of Northumberland. Chambers was hanged at the gallows outside the city walls at the Knavesmire. Another man with the name of Bladis was hanged, drawn and quartered on the Pavement in the centre of York, while a local man called Warton was hanged at one of the points where the rebels had gained entry into the city.

While he was in York and in Bishopthorpe, Henry also pardoned a large number of rebels. The Great Chronicle of London states many people *"fearing grievous punishment, put halters about their necks, and in their shirts came into a great court of the palace where the King was lodged, and there kneeling cried lamentably for mercy and grace, to whom at length the King granted forgiveness and pardon"*.

It appears one of the men who was pardoned was Alderman Wrangwyshe. He must have felt he was a lucky man indeed. With the rebellion routed, the leaders dead and some of its followers pardoned, Henry summoned his army together and marched them south. He never returned to York again.

For a time, King Henry looked to his Council of the North to maintain order on the crown's behalf across the North of England, including in York, Yorkshire and beyond. However, after a few years, the influence of the Council began to wane and it ceased to function in any meaningful way. After this, the Council of the North lay dormant for several decades before being re-established in the 1530's during the latter years of the reign of Henry VIII.

CHAPTER FIVE
Riots and Child Marriages

Although York was no longer a focal point for major rebellion, it would be wrong to think the city didn't have troubles and times of unrest during the remainder of Henry VII's time on the throne. As previously outlined in the book's introduction, York was in the middle of a long-term decline. Wool processing had all but ceased and the city's position as one of the north's major trading centres was fading away. Records of illness during Henry's reign are hard to come by but there were certainly outbreaks of plague and other diseases.

The local population was also not averse to starting the odd riot. A number of major outbreaks of violence were caused by York's citizens' disgruntlement with the Church for allowing its animals to graze on areas of common land while their own stock was prevented from doing so.

The enclosure disturbances in York reached their zenith in 1495 when the King felt the need to summon the Lord Mayor and several other of the Corporation's officials all the way from York to Greenwich Palace outside London. The men from the north were left in no doubt of what might happen if they allowed the troubles in their home city to continue.

Henry railed at them, "*I may not see the city go into utter ruin and decay in default of you that should rule, for rather if necessary, I must and will put in other rulers that will rule and govern the city according to my laws.*"

Thomas Howard, the Earl of Surrey was requested to act in

a mediation role between the locals and the officials of the Church. Thankfully, Surrey managed to calm the situation down sufficiently and the Corporation's officials remained in place.

Domestic matters in Tudor York were often similar to those in many other towns and cities at the time. One custom which perhaps wasn't widely commonplace but did occur now and then was the very dubious practice of childhood marriage. Often the rationale for such a union was a child's family's desire to gain financially or socially.

In 1497, Alderman William Nelson married his daughter Katherine to William Gascoigne, the son of a wealthy local gentleman. Katherine's age isn't recorded but William was nine. The *"couple"* lived at Katherine's father's house for five years before they eventually moved into a home of their own, although Gascoigne later deserted his young wife.

Other examples of this practice include two daughters of the York official George Ewers. He married off one of the poor girls when she was twelve and the other when she was only six, this time to another member of the Gascoigne family. There was also the *"marriage"* of John Norman, aged eight, and Barbara Wentworth, when she was just five or six years old. We'll examine the implications of this union for one of York's future Archbishops later in the book.

However, we shouldn't think the practice was widespread. During the Tudor period the majority of people in York married for the first time around the age of twenty. Due to the high rates of mortality in the city, remarriages were common. Many people had a second, third or even fourth husband or wife.

The year of 1503 brought with it a brief interlude in York's troubles, and there was another opportunity for the city to hold a right royal celebration. The King's second child Margaret Tudor had been born in the Palace of Westminster in 1489. To strengthen the relationship between the two countries, an agreement had been made that Margaret should marry James IV, the King of Scotland.

The formal marriage ceremony was set to take place in Edinburgh in the summer of 1503. However, six months earlier, the two had been wed in a so-called proxy ceremony (James wasn't present) in Richmond Palace. James had been thirty years old and Margaret thirteen. It appears child marriages were also popular with royalty.

In July 1503, Margaret set off from Richmond accompanied by the Earl of Surrey and a large supporting entourage. On the journey north, the Queen of Scotland's progress was rather like an East Coast mainline train. The group stopped at Grantham, Newark and Doncaster, before entering the Vale of York by crossing the river Wharfe at Tadcaster.

When Queen Margaret's party finally arrived in York, they were greeted by the latest Earl of Northumberland (the previous murdered Earl's son Henry Percy) and many of his supporters. A mass of Corporation officials and citizens also lined the city's streets. By the time the parade had reached Micklegate Bar, the crowd had swelled so much that the royal procession was struggling to gain access through the wide-open gates.

Queen Margaret's immediate party were housed in buildings which were connected to St Mary's Abbey (also known as York Abbey). A few years earlier in 1497, a small archway and gate had been built into the abbey walls near Bootham Bar. After her visit, this entry point was renamed Queen Margaret's Arch in honour of the Queen of Scotland's brief stay in the city.

Although the adjacent walls have long since been demolished, the archway is still standing in the centre of York. If you visit today, you'll be able to read the following (if not totally accurate) inscription:

"This Gateway was broken through the Abbey Wall July 1503 in honour of the Princess Margaret daughter of Henry VII,

who was the guest of the Lord Abbot of St Mary's for two days on her journey to the North as the Bride of James IV of Scotland."

Following Queen Margaret's arrival in the city, the Corporation of York's officials once again hosted lavish royal celebrations.

"This year, on the 14th of July, the Lady Margaret, Elder Daughter of the King, and Queen of Scots, accompanied with many lords, knights and ladies, came to this city whereby the Mayor, Aldermen, Sheriffs and Citizens, they were most honourably entertained."

After leaving York, the royal progress carried on its way north through Berwick-upon-Tweed and travelled on until Edinburgh. Here, the royal couple were finally married in person in a formal ceremony held at Holyrood Abbey on 8 August. One of their future children would become the next King of Scotland, James V.

This James would have a daughter, who would be known down the ages as Mary Queen of Scots. Mary in turn would give birth to a baby boy called James Stuart who, in time, would grow up to be both King James VI of Scotland and King James I of England. James' visit to York in 1603 would coincide with the end of the Tudor dynasty but we'll return to that nearer to the end of the book.

Henry VII died of tuberculosis in the year 1509. In his will, the first Tudor King of England left behind a substantial legacy of 20,000 marks (a mark was a common term used for an amount of money equal to two-thirds of a pound) for a new hospital to be built in his memory in York. This was a very positive gesture. Unfortunately, the money wasn't forthcoming and the hospital was never built.

CHAPTER SIX
Henry VIII - The Early Years

Henry VII's heir had previously been set to be his elder son, Prince Arthur. The untimely death of the Prince of Wales in 1502 changed all that. Instead, the country's new ruler would be Henry's second son and namesake. When Henry VIII came to the throne in 1509, he was just seventeen. One of his first acts as monarch of England was to marry his brother's widow, Catherine of Aragon. The future undoing of their union would have a significant implication for York in the years to come.

At the beginning of Henry VIII's reign, the new King was predominantly looking outwards to the north at Scotland and across the English Channel to Europe, where expensive wars were being fought with the French. For a while, Henry had little time to think about a northern city like York, other than as a useful source of taxation, income and fighting men.

York though did act as a stopping off point for some of Henry's soldiers on their way north to fight against Scotland. In 1513, following the defeat of the Scots at Flodden Field, the city acted as a staging post for a body travelling in the opposite direction.

After her brief visit to York in 1503, Margaret Tudor had travelled northwards to Edinburgh to meet her new husband, King James IV of Scotland. Her father's ambition had been to solidify the relationship between their two nations. It didn't work. A decade later in 1513, Margaret's husband declared war on England in support of Scotland's alliance with France. The announcement came as little surprise to Margaret's younger brother. Henry VIII appears to have been expecting it. He ordered his forces in the north to engage with the Scots' army, which was being led in person by Henry's sister's husband James.

In his rallying cry to the Scots, James IV made a bold claim that they would soon capture York. It wasn't to be. Shortly afterwards, the Scots king was killed in the battle of Flodden Field, not far from where the English border with Scotland is today, some fifteen miles southwest of Berwick-upon-Tweed. In doing so, he became the last British monarch (at least to date) to die in battle. James' body was embalmed in Newcastle and transported south to Sheen Priory near Richmond Upon Thames. One of the resting places of his royal corpse during this journey was a stopover in York.

Life in the city continued to be hard for most of York's population, with sporadic outbreaks of rioting and unrest. One thing York did have going for it though, of course, was the sheer number of important religious houses located there. In Tudor times, as today, one major religious building dominated York's skyline, the mother church and the cathedral of the diocese, York Minster. The Minster was also the seat of the second most important churchman in the whole of England.

Despite this, during the early decades of the Tudors, some of the Archbishops of York spent very little time in the city. We'll shine a spotlight onto one of these men, Thomas Wolsey, shortly. Later on in the book, we'll also examine the actions of a number of Wolsey's successors.

The Minster was a home to numerous chantries, chapels and canonries. Chantries were usually small chapels or parts of a larger church dedicated to the singing of Mass for the soul of the founder of the chantry or others. They were typically funded by an endowment established by the chantry's founder and/or other donations.

Many of the canons notionally located in York Minster held lucrative positions linked to large revenue generating estates owned by the Church. Some of these men were as equally absent from York as their Archbishop. In contrast, a large number of clergymen and other Church officials did work in York Minster and in the surrounding buildings. The most senior of these was the man responsible for overseeing the Minster's governance, the Dean of York.

In Tudor York, the Church operated a number of ecclesiastical courts and employed a wide range of lawyers and other legal officials. Based at the Minster, the Church also had its own legal jurisdiction known as the Liberty of St Peter. Law and justice were managed separately there from in the rest of the city. The Liberty managed its own gaol, called the Peter Prison, and had a specialist police force. While the Peter Prison was closed in the nineteenth century, the Minster constabulary still exists today. The modern remit though focuses mostly on safety and security, rather than on law and order which these days is managed by the civil police.

The second most important religious establishment in York at the beginning of the Tudor period was St Mary's Abbey, sometimes referred to as York Abbey. Led by an abbot and run by Benedictine monks, St Mary's was one of the ten richest monasteries in the whole of England. As we've seen, St Mary's was even grand and wealthy enough to be able to host King Henry VII's daughter Queen Margaret of Scotland as she travelled north to meet her new husband in Edinburgh. Then as now, royal visits didn't come cheap.

Another important and sizeable building was St Leonard's Hospital. Located at a site adjacent to St Mary's but within the city walls, St Leonard's was one of the largest hospitals in England. At times during the reign of Henry VIII, the religious men and nurses of St Leonard's had the capacity to care for the physical and spiritual needs of over two hundred people, including a plethora of poor, ill and elderly patients.

York also played host to a variety of other religious houses. These included:

- The Gilbertine priory of St Andrew - next to the river Foss and Fishergate,
- The Benedictine priory of Holy Trinity - located at the top of Micklegate,
- The Austin or Augustinian friary - on Lendal,
- The Franciscan Grey friary - situated between Castlegate and the river Ouse,
- The Dominican Black friary - in North Street,
- The Carmelite White friary - off Fossgate, and
- St Clement's Benedictine priory and nunnery - located just outside the city walls above the banks of the Ouse near to where Nunnery Lane is today.

On top of all this, there were a number of smaller chapels and chantries and numerous (approximately forty) parish churches. Far too many it might seem for York's reduced population.

If you can create a mental picture then of Tudor York, it's easy to imagine just how much of the land in the city was owned by the Church and populated by the religious establishments. In addition, much of the domestic housing stock in York around this time was owned by the religious houses, both those based in York and elsewhere in the country. Rent paid by York householders had been providing a steady enough income for the Church for a number of generations.

One clear inference of the above is that the Church was a major landowner and an economic powerhouse in early Tudor York. After everything else which had befallen the city and led to its declining population and wealth, at least the Corporation and York's population could rely on the Church to buy from their merchants, spend in their markets and hire their labour to build, clean, cook and make repairs. If this, or much of it, was to be lost, York would be in trouble.

#

Despite all the income being generated by the Church from the religious houses and the employment of what at times must have seemed like an army of clerical and lay staff, York continued to struggle economically. During the first half of the sixteenth century, the Corporation was often facing a seemingly endless struggle to balance the books. As a consequence, repeated calls were made to King Henry and his officials to reduce the tax burden placed on the city.

When taxes had to be raised, there were limited sources where the money could come from. Rents and tolls and other incomes could only go so far. Although there were wealthy people in the city, including the aldermen, who could be taxed and were, many amongst York's population were much poorer. Some were even destitute. Institutions such as St Leonard's Hospital and the forty parish churches did what they could for the infirm and the poor, but the problem was significant.

York, like many other early Tudor towns and cities, had a significant begging problem. During the reign of King Henry VII, the 1494 Vagabonds and Beggars Act had legislated that *"vagabonds, idle and suspected persons"* could be placed in the stocks for up to three days and fed only bread and water, before being sent back home to where they came from.

During the first decade of Henry VIII's reign, the Corporation had begun to characterise York's beggars into two distinct groups. The first they adjudged as being *"mighty of body"*. If such people were caught begging they were to be punished in line with the law. The second group, however, were classified as being sick or infirm. People falling into this category garnered more sympathy. From time to time, the Corporation even issued *"tokens"* for selected people to display on their shoulder. The wearing of these badges allowed infirm men and women in York to beg openly on the city's streets without fear of arrest or official punishment.

Against this backdrop of a continued fall in population, declining revenues and licensed and unlicensed beggars on the streets, it's little surprise there were sometimes bouts of unrest in the city. From time to time, these became quite serious. In 1514, news of one such outbreak travelled as far south as London.

We don't know exactly what happened because the Corporation opted not to include details of the rioting in the city's records, but the troubles were severe enough for Henry VIII to feel he had no choice but to intervene. The King declared prompt action had to be taken against the *"enormities"* which had been committed in the city. The Corporation was forced to send William Nelson, an alderman and former Member of Parliament, south to represent them at the King's Council. Nelson was given a dressing down, as were the rest of the colleagues by proxy in their absence, for failing to keep order.

Subsequently the Corporation of York decided their city needed a champion, someone who could speak up for York in the royal court. The man they targeted for this role was Thomas Wolsey, the newly appointed Archbishop of York. Wolsey's predecessor Cardinal Christopher Bainbridge had spent little time in Yorkshire. Perhaps he would have been wise to have spent more time there. He was murdered in Rome in 1514, having been poisoned by a priest who was also his steward.

Thomas Wolsey was a man on the up. Over time, he'd been playing an increasingly important role in both the Church and the English state. His position as one of the King's closest and most trusted advisors was borne out in 1515 when Henry appointed him as the new Lord Chancellor of England. As such, Wolsey was the most senior minister in the English government. In the same year, Pope Leo X made him a Cardinal of the Catholic Church.

Despite his undoubted importance to the history of England, it's a fair question to ask about whether Thomas Wolsey should feature at all in a history book about Tudor York. In the fifteen years which followed his appointment as Archbishop, Wolsey didn't once visit the city. He didn't even travel to Yorkshire. For most of this time, he was focused on matters of national importance rather than regional significance. However, the Archbishop's busy schedule and his physical absence from York didn't stop him from making a difference.

Soon after he became Archbishop, Wolsey began to take an active interest in York's wellbeing. One of the first tasks he undertook was in 1516, when he opted to intervene on the city's behalf in a serious rift between two factions of the Corporation.

An election had recently taken place in York to appoint a new alderman. The result had been a tie between the two candidates. One of the men, William Cure, had been a Sheriff of York in 1511, while the other, John Norman, had served more recently as a Sheriff in 1514. Since then both men had served the Corporation as members of the Twenty-Four.

The existing aldermen's support for the two candidates was split down the middle. The outgoing Lord Mayor was a wealthy York image maker and carver called Thomas Drawswerd. He and half of York's aldermen had championed John Norman. The other half were being led by Alderman William Nelson. This was the man who'd been told off by the King's Council. Nelson and his faction had thrown their weight behind William Cure.

Neither Thomas Drawswerd nor William Nelson had an unblemished reputation. You might not remember it (I appreciate there are a lot of names in this book) but we've come across

William Nelson before. He was the man who oversaw the childhood marriage of his own daughter Katherine to William Gascoigne.

In the early 1500's, he was twice asked to become a knight (due to his income rather than for any specific noble act) but twice turned it down and was fined. It appears some people weren't fans of the honours system even back in those days. Nelson was fined again in 1503, but this time it was for threatening the Lord Mayor of York. He certainly seems to have been a colourful character, although perhaps at times not one you'd necessarily like to meet. Having said that, he also represented York in four different Parliaments.

William Nelson knew Thomas Drawswerd very well. In addition to having served York together as aldermen, they'd both represented the city during the Parliament of 1512. There's some speculation on the History of Parliament website that during his time as an MP, Drawswerd may have used his position to try and win contracts for himself related to the construction of Henry VII's promised hospital in York. If he did this, he wasn't in luck. Neither the contract nor the funds to build the hospital ever materialised.

Perhaps the two men just didn't like each other. Whatever the reason, it appears they had no appetite for compromise. As their positions hardened, other people began to take sides. It wasn't long before another bout of violence was breaking out on York's streets. Reports were made of *"diverse great riots and affrays"* between the two factions.

When word of the new outbreak of disorder reached London, it was decided that the situation was serious enough to merit another formal intervention by the national government. Archbishop Wolsey stepped forward and summoned both Drawswerd and Nelson to London to attend a session of the Royal Council. After the situation in York was described and analysed, a ruling was laid down that neither of the two nominated men, Norman nor Cure, should be elected as an alderman. In addition, the city's representatives were told that no other aldermen were to be elected in York without Wolsey's express permission.

After the hearing, Drawswerd was allowed to return north to Yorkshire. Nelson though was arrested and locked up in Fleet gaol. It appears he and, perhaps to a lesser extent, William Cure may have been adjudged to have been responsible for the disturbances in York.

Not long afterwards another alderman died, and a second vacancy became available. The existing aldermen decided the best way to resolve their differences would be to elect both Norman and Cure to fill the gaps. They also made a decision that despite the fact he was still in prison, Alderman Nelson should be elected to serve for a second term as Lord Mayor.

Wolsey was unable to prevent Henry VIII from hearing about the appointments made in York. The King was furious. He wrote an angry letter to the Corporation informing them of his *"great displeasure"* at their actions. The elevations of the two new prospective aldermen were quickly rescinded, and alternative candidates elected in their place. Thomas Wolsey also wrote to the Corporation to tell them the King's orders must be actioned in full. Once again, the aldermen acted quickly. Only a day after his letter had reached them, John Dodgson was made the new Lord Mayor elect in place of William Nelson.

When eventually Alderman Nelson was finally released from prison, he'd had his fill of politics. Already a rich man, with properties in Acaster Malbis, Grimston, Kelfield and Riccall, he didn't stand for either Parliament or Lord Mayor again. When he returned home to Yorkshire, he resigned his position at the Corporation, moved away from York and retired to a country house in Riccall.

In contrast, Thomas Drawswerd retained his place on the Corporation and served a second term as Lord Mayor in 1523. Surviving property taxation records show he was one of the richest men in York by the mid 1520's. At the time of his death in 1529, his estate included nine houses and tenements which were spread out across several different districts in York.

Eventually, the two candidates who'd initially been barred from office, John Norman and William Cure, were both elected as aldermen in the same year of 1521. Presumably by then the dust had settled, or Henry VIII had more important matters to worry about.

John Norman was a rich merchant. It was his son Anthony who had married Barbara Wentworth at the age of eight. Alderman Norman went on to become one of the wealthiest men in the whole of York. He served the city as one of its Members of Parliament in 1523 and as Lord Mayor in 1524. The latter role was in succession to the man who'd championed him, Thomas Drawswerd.

When John Norman died only a year later in 1525, he left behind a range of properties in York, Ripon and Doncaster. He also bequeathed a small amount of money to York's friaries, hospitals and prisons.

Despite the riots and troubles of 1516, Thomas Wolsey declared his *"great love and good mind"* for the city of York. In the coming years, he spoke out a number of times in favour of Corporation at the royal court and acted upon the city's behalf whenever he could. For example, in 1523 Wolsey played a pivotal role in negotiations with King Henry to ensure York gained a monopoly on the export of all of the wool which was produced across most of Yorkshire. This was a considerable coup for the city and was very well regarded by York's merchants and traders. Wolsey also acted several times to support the Corporation in its attempts to reduce the city's fee farm tax or to prevent it from rising any further.

By 1529, however, things had begun to turn sour for Wolsey. His fall from grace was closely aligned to the refusal of the Catholic Church to make a decision about the annulment of Henry VIII's marriage to his first wife Catherine of Aragon. The Church's failure to do so didn't go down at all well with Henry. Egged on by some of Wolsey's enemies, the King became convinced Thomas Wolsey was at least partially to blame.

Wolsey was replaced as Lord Chancellor and forced to leave his official offices and properties, including Hampton Court. He did, however, maintain his position in the Church as the Archbishop of York. With the tide turning so strongly against him in London, Wolsey travelled north to the relative safety and sanctuary of his diocese. Finally, the Minster once again had an Archbishop of York in residence, although Wolsey spent the majority of his time in the Church's nearby palace at Cawood. Perhaps to take his mind off his troubles, the Archbishop set about restoring the palace to its former glory.

In 1530, while still in Cawood, Thomas Wolsey was accused of high treason and arrested by Henry Percy, the Earl of Northumberland. During the journey back to the south of England for Wolsey's trial and likely execution, the Archbishop fell ill. Thomas Wolsey died in Leicester. Like Richard III before him, he was buried there, although not at the time in an unmarked grave.

These days though a mystery remains. Exactly where is Thomas Wolsey's body? It's known he was buried in the grounds of Leicester's Augustinian Abbey, but nobody knows the exact location of his last resting place. Despite repeated attempts and several excavations to locate them, (at the time of writing) Wolsey's remains have yet to been found.

The Catholic Church's failure to allow King Henry VIII to divorce Catherine of Aragon and marry Anne Boleyn was to have serious consequences, not least for York. Although Thomas Wolsey had repeatedly acted to help the city during his lifetime, he'd no longer be around to protect it from what might happen next.

CHAPTER SEVEN
The Dissolution and Pilgrimage of Grace

With Archbishop Wolsey no longer in a position or even alive to support them, the Corporation decided to seek help from another source. The man they targeted for this was one of Wolsey's closest supporters, Thomas Cromwell. The aldermen assigned one of their own colleagues to gain Cromwell's backing.

Sir George Lawson was already one of the richest men in York. With his sphere of influence extending far beyond the city walls, he was a good choice for the role. In years gone by, he'd served his nation in Tournai in modern day Belgium after it had been captured by Henry VIII's army. He'd also held just about every job under the sun in the border garrison town of Berwick-upon-Tweed. His roles there had included deputy captain, bridgemaster, master carpenter, master mason, master of the ordnance, receiver and treasurer.

In 1516, Lawson joined the Corpus Christi religious guild in York. By 1527, he'd been elected as an alderman. Around this time, he also became an official of the Council of the North. In 1530, he was elected to serve his first term as Lord Mayor of York, before twice going on to become one of the city's Members of Parliament.

Using his connections and his powers of persuasion, Lawson persuaded Cromwell to support York on a number of issues. Perhaps the most important of these was the ongoing thorny issue of the city's tax burden. In 1536, Cromwell's intervention was crucial in ensuring a new act of Parliament was passed. After many failed attempts, the act finally formally reduced the city's annual fee farm taxation payment. No doubt when word reached York, the aldermen would have shared a tankard or two to celebrate.

Another key issue facing York was trade. During the previous decades, navigation along the river Ouse between York and the port of Hull via the Humber had become increasingly problematic. Cromwell acted to ensure vital improvements were not just signed off but designed and finally made to this route which was so vital to the city's imports and exports.

However, most of York's aldermen would have been in despair if they'd known what else Thomas Cromwell was planning. There was about to be a significant shift in the balance of power in England between the Church and the state, and Cromwell would have a key role to play in this. In addition, the implications for York would be significant.

At this point, it's worth quickly examining affairs at a national level before we focus our attention back down on York. Over the years, Henry VIII had become increasingly concerned about the lack of a legitimate son and male heir to his throne. By the end of the 1520's, he no longer believed his wife Catherine of Aragon (the mother of his daughter Mary) could provide this. As this was the case, he began to look elsewhere, particularly in the direction of Anne Boleyn.

Much to Catherine's disdain, Henry and his officials began to make requests to the Pope to annul their marriage. The pontiff Pope Clement VII found himself in a tricky position. He didn't want to upset such an important Catholic monarch but if he agreed to Henry's request, he'd have to undo a controversial ruling which had been laid down by one of his predecessors Pope Julius II in 1503.

The issue back then had been related to Catherine's brief marriage to Henry's brother Arthur. In the Bible, Leviticus argues that a man should not be permitted to wed his brother's widow. It appears this could have barred Henry from marrying Catherine. However, when the case was heard in 1503, Pope Julius gave the couple special dispensation for their wedding to go ahead. This was on the basis that Catherine's marriage to Arthur had never been consummated.

Decades later, Henry and his advisors began to claim this was an error. Despite repeated requests for the Pope to make a decision, Clement continued to procrastinate. Eventually, Henry began to give up all hope of achieving Papal approval. Encouraged by his increasingly influential advisor (and friend of York) Thomas Cromwell, the King concluded the only way he'd get the decision to fall in his favour would be if it was made closer to home. Consequently, Henry decided the Church in England had to break away from Rome.

Once this momentous decision was made, things happened quickly. In 1533, Henry married Anne Boleyn. A new act of Parliament was passed. This stated the final say on all legal and religious matters in England was down to the King. The newly appointed Archbishop of Canterbury Thomas Cranmer held a special hearing to consider Henry's marital status. He issued a decree stating that the Papal dispensation which had legalised Henry and Catherine's marriage in the first place was flawed and invalid. As a result it was confirmed, in English law at any rate, that Henry was legally married to Anne Boleyn. Shortly afterwards in September 1533, Anne gave birth to a daughter. In the coming years, the baby girl would grow up to be Queen Elizabeth I.

With the annulment achieved, Henry was minded to mend England's fractured relationship with the Vatican. However, his plans were foiled in 1534, when Pope Clement finally made up his mind about Henry and Catherine's union. He proclaimed it remained valid. As a result, the Church in Rome considered

Henry's second marriage to Anne was illegal. The King of England was furious.

An Act of Supremacy was soon passed in the English Parliament which confirmed the monarch, rather than the Pope, was the true head of the Church of England. The act also stated that the King *"shall have and enjoy ... all honours, dignities, pre-eminences, jurisdictions, privileges, authorities, immunities, profits and commodities to the said dignity of the supreme head of the same Church."*

In 1535, Henry appointed Thomas Cromwell to be his *"Vice-Gerent in spirituals"*. From this time onwards until his death, Cromwell was the King's deputy in all matters related to the Church. His ecclesiastical powers and jurisdiction exceeded even that of the archbishops.

Although Henry had no particular wish to see the practices of the Church change, he had expensive tastes, a country to run and costly wars to fight. The Church was by far the wealthiest institution in the country, much richer even than the crown. The legal right to *"have and enjoy"* its *"profits and commodities"* was just too good an opportunity for the King to turn down. Someone though would be needed to make this possible.

Thomas Cromwell created a plan for the *"Visitation"* to be carried out across the country. This was a new variant on a traditional process where a bishop or other leader of a religious order would visit and inspect the institutions within their jurisdiction. This time though the inspectors would be selected by and report to Cromwell.

The Visitation's commissioners were tasked with auditing the financial assets of each and every house of religion in England and Wales. Once identified, their assets were to be recorded in the *"Valor Ecclesiasticus"*. This was a new national ledger created to make a detailed record of the Church's wealth.

Over the coming months, Cromwell's officers visited

virtually every religious house in the country. In York, they spent much of their time in St Mary's Abbey, St Leonard's Hospital and the smaller priories and friaries. The local commissioners selected for the Visitation included Cromwell's confidante and York alderman Sir George Lawson. Working with his associates, Lawson identified and recorded the land, assets and income of each of the religious houses. The abbots, nuns and friars across York and elsewhere in the country assisted rather unenthusiastically. Some of them must have suspected and feared what might happen next.

As they went about their business investigating the religious houses, the Visitation's commissioners were also tasked with uncovering as many financial, moral and other improprieties they could find linked to the staff and brethren in each of the houses. Cromwell wanted a record of these, just in case they might become useful should anyone challenge his future plans.

In York, a series of accusations were recorded. These included sexual offences alleged to have been committed by thirteen monks and one brother at St Leonard's. The commissioners also noted that many of the monks, brothers and nuns in York's religious houses harboured wishes to leave their orders in future.

In 1536, the Suppression of Religious Houses Act or the Act for the Dissolution of the Lesser Monasteries was passed through Parliament. This act decreed that all the religious houses with an annual income of less than £200 should be dissolved. The only exception to this rule was to be if a special exemption was granted by the King. The assets from each of these houses were to be sold off if possible and transferred to the Crown.

Across the country, in the region of three hundred religious houses were adjudged to have fallen within the scope of the classification. They included three houses in York. With their names on the list, St Andrew's, Holy Trinity and St Clement's were all scheduled to be asset stripped and closed down during the summer of 1536.

St Andrew's however was part of the Gilbertine Order. The master of the Gilbertines at this time was Robert Holgate. We'll hear more about Holgate later as he would go to become one of York's future Archbishops. Most of the Gilbertine houses across England, including St Andrew's in York, were relatively small. With an annual income of less than £200, each of them found themselves within scope of the proposed dissolution.

Robert Holgate, however, maintained a positive relationship with Thomas Cromwell. A clever man, he used this influence to gain a special exemption for each of the Gilbertine houses under his mastership. At least in the short term, every one of them, including St Andrew's, was allowed to remain open.

The other houses in York and right across the country though which had been earmarked for closure were re-visited by Cromwell's commissioners. The ecclesiastical staff were instructed to move out. All the valuable assets, such as items made of gold and silver, were collected and removed. The lead was lifted and taken down from the roofs and other precious metals stripped from their locations. Many saleable items of lower value were auctioned off locally. Most of the properties and their land were sold, leased or rented.

The initial focus in York was on the two Benedictine houses of Holy Trinity and St Clement's. As part of the transfer of these houses' assets to the crown, both sites were leased. The two men who sought to profit from these leases were perhaps rather unsurprisingly friends of Sir George Lawson. William Maunsell took control of St Clement's, while Leonard Beckwith leased out Holy Trinity. In August 1536, St Clement's was closed. Holy Trinity soon followed.

The dissolution of so many of the smaller religious houses allied with some of Cromwell's other policies began to create a public outcry, particularly in the more conservative parts of the country such as the northern counties of England. Several protests were held in York, but these were soon overshadowed by a series of much larger rebellions.

One of the most significant of these, the Pilgrimage of Grace, began its life in earnest in Beverley in the East Riding of Yorkshire. Within weeks, the uprising's leader, the lawyer Robert Aske, had gathered together a force of around nine thousand men. They set off and marched towards the regional capital of York.

The Lord Mayor of York at this time was William Harrington. Originally a grocer, Harrington had also served as the bailiff for York's ecclesiastical jurisdiction. Widowed twice, he'd been married three times. His later marriages provide good examples of the sometimes quite complex relationships which existed between the families of Corporation officials. Harrington's second wife was the widow of a fellow alderman. When she died and Harrington married again, his third wife was another alderman's daughter.

One of William Harrington's own daughters Jane married yet another alderman, the merchant Robert Hall who would go on to become Lord Mayor of York in 1541 and 1557 and one of York's Members of Parliament on two separate occasions.

When Harrington's other daughter Ellen was wed, she married a legal official in the Church called William Fawkes. The couple had a son called Edward. Edward would go on to become a legal officer for the by then Protestant Church of England. He and his wife Edith would have a son called Guy. Perhaps we'll return to consider Guy Fawkes in a future chapter.

In 1536 as Robert Aske and thousands of *"pilgrims"* approached York, tensions were running high. On 14 October, Lord Mayor Harrington and Alderman Lawson wrote a joint letter to the King pleading with him to provide support for the city against the incoming force. Their request was sent and received too late. Popular feeling in the city had already turned by this time and was now favouring the rebels.

On 16 October 1536, with such a large force approaching York, the city's leaders believed they had little choice but to open the gates. Robert Aske and his followers were allowed inside. As the pilgrims' leaders entered the central area of York, Aske acted swiftly to prevent the city from being looted and ransacked. He made orders that the majority of his men were to remain outside the walls, and that all goods and services consumed were to be paid for.

Aske also made a proclamation, in which he explained the rationale for the Pilgrims' actions, *"For this pilgrimage, we have taken for the preservation of Christ's church, of this realm of England, the King our sovereign lord, the nobility and commons of the same..."*

As he presented the rebels' arguments to Lord Mayor Harrington, Aske stated, *"By the suppression of so many religious houses the service of God is not well performed, and the poor are unrelieved"*.

When Robert Aske arrived at York Minster, he was greeted there by a group of senior clergymen. There was at least one notable absentee from the ecclesiastical delegation. Thomas Wolsey's successor as Archbishop of York, Edward Lee, had already fled from York to the relative safety of Pontefract Castle.

After an Evensong service was heard at the Minster, Aske nailed a series of orders onto the great wooden doors. These stated that all religious houses which had been closed down were to be reopened and all the monks and nuns reinstated and welcomed back to their previous positions and homes.

The picture of what happened next is slightly confusing, particularly in terms of the somewhat ambiguous position which had been adopted by Sir George Lawson. He was, after all, the man in the city with the closest connections to the pilgrims' nemesis Thomas Cromwell. Even though Lawson had been one of the Visitation's commissioners and had leased out York's closed religious house to two of his friends, when Robert Aske arrived in York, Lawson greeted him personally. He welcomed Aske into his own home and asked him to stay there while he was in York. Whether this was down to some newfound ideological commitment to the Pilgrimage of Grace, or possibly for reasons of self-preservation, I'll let you decide.

In the coming weeks, a number of the religious houses in the northern counties which had been closed over the summer were reopened. In York, the monks who'd been turfed unceremoniously out of Holy Trinity a few months earlier returned to their positions. The house of Leonard Beckwith, the man who'd taken on the lease of the priory's land and buildings, was ransacked by the rebels. Fearing for his life, Beckwith fled and escaped from York.

The Benedictine monks and nuns displaced from St Clement's were also welcomed back into their priory. The lessee at St Clement's, William Maunsell, made a different decision to Beckwith. He didn't leave York. Instead, he kept his head down. It appears he may have had a lucky escape. During the subsequent inquiry to investigate the Pilgrimage of Grace, Maunsell testified the rebels had been planning to murder him.

Clearly there was trouble in the air. To prevent another act of violence, Alderman Lawson advised one of his friends who was the treasurer at the Minster to take down Cromwell's coat of arms from over his door. If this had not been done swiftly, the threat which had been made to burn the building down may well have been carried out. This would have been a particular shame, as these days the Treasurer's House is an excellent National Trust property.

Although Robert Aske remained in York for only four days,

some of the rebels continued to use the city as a base for much longer. On 20 October, the Earl of Northumberland's brother Sir Thomas Percy who'd thrown his lot in with the rebels, led a large parade of pilgrims through the centre of the city. At the head of the march, Percy walked alongside the abbot of St Mary's Abbey, although it was later reported that the abbot had been a reluctant guest in proceedings. Or perhaps this was just a story the abbot told afterwards.

As Aske led the main body of his men south towards Doncaster, their numbers swelled even further. Some estimates state at one stage there were around thirty thousand men, which is a huge number given the population at the time. A few weeks later they encountered a much smaller English army, roughly about a third of their own size, being led by the Duke of Norfolk and the Earl of Shrewsbury.

Heavily outnumbered, Norfolk was forced to negotiate. Following initial talks between the pilgrims and the King's representatives near Doncaster, a major conference was held in Pontefract Castle. At this meeting, the pilgrims presented a list of their demands to Norfolk with instructions for them to be passed on to the King. The city of York was formally represented at the conference by a small delegation. Interestingly this included Sir George Lawson, although later he claimed he'd been ill and had missed most of the proceedings.

Norfolk agreed with the rebels that the closure of any additional religious houses should be halted until Parliament had sat without any interference from the King. In addition, many of the rebels' wider demands were also agreed to, including a commitment for Parliament to sit in York at some stage during the coming year. The pilgrims' leaders and their followers were promised pardons. Having reached what they believed to be a fair and equable agreement, Aske and the other leaders stood their men down.

As the pilgrims waited for the promises made to them to be fulfilled, there was a separate outbreak of unrest in other parts of the North of England in February 1537. Although the new activities weren't directly related to the Pilgrimage of Grace, the crown used the unrest as a pretence to move against the pilgrims' leaders. Robert Aske and many others, including several leading churchmen associated with the Pilgrimage of Grace, were rounded up and placed into custody. Of those arrested, many laymen, including Sir Thomas Percy, and several churchmen were soon tried and executed.

Robert Aske was transported south and held prisoner in the Tower of London, before being taken to Westminster and placed on trial. Although Aske was found guilty of high treason, he wasn't executed, at least not immediately. Instead, Henry VIII decided the people of the North needed to witness a demonstration of what would happen to treacherous rebels.

Aske was transported back to York at the King's request. According to Henry, this was where his prisoner had been in *"his greatest and most frantic glory"*. A such, it was where he should also die.

On a market day during the summer of 1537, Robert Aske was publicly hanged in chains at York Castle next to Clifford's Tower. A fortnight later, Lord Hussey of Duffield and William Wode, the Prior of Bridlington, were taken to the gallows at the Knavesmire and hanged, drawn and quartered for the same crime of high treason, due to their own support for the Pilgrimage of Grace. Robert Aske's body was later taken down and placed on public display at nearby Heworth Moor.

The Corporation of York had already taken action to limit the damage which might be done to the city's reputation due to its links with the rebels. All records of major Corporation meetings held between October and December 1536 were either exceptionally brief, erased or had not been made in the first place.

Despite having displayed some apparent sympathy for Robert Aske and the pilgrims' cause, Alderman Lawson managed to avoid arrest. Rather conveniently, he decided to spend some time out of the limelight in Berwick-upon-Tweed. Shortly before Robert Aske's execution, the Earl of Norfolk confirmed in a letter to Thomas Cromwell that Lawson remained trustworthy and was loyal to the crown.

The Earl added that a man like Lawson would be very useful for the authorities to have in the North. However, the other officials of the Corporation of York and the city's population in general realised their reputation had been sullied in the eyes of the King. They waited nervously to see what Henry VIII might do next.

CHAPTER EIGHT
Economic Disaster for York

With the Pilgrimage of Grace quashed and its leaders dead, Thomas Cromwell began to introduce a number of gradual reforms to the Church. The King in contrast focused much of his time on more domestic matters. Having delivered Henry VIII a daughter rather than a son, Ann Boleyn was eventually executed. In 1537, the King's third wife Jane Seymour blessed him with the legitimate son and heir he'd longed for. Sadly, Jane Seymour died only two weeks later after giving birth to Prince Edward.

Under Thomas Cromwell's direction, a series of changes were introduced to church services and practices. Often, these weren't popular. Sometimes they were even ignored in parts of religiously traditional areas, including in northern towns and cities like York.

Although some of the reforms were delayed or blocked due to debates with the bishops, a few did move ahead. Minor feast days were changed from holidays to working days. Pilgrimages were discouraged. Religious relics were banned, and instructions were issued that relics, which were considered to be superstitious, should be removed from the churches.

Cromwell also made an order that each parish should create and maintain an accurate register of baptisms, marriages and burials. Family historians and many others have much to thank Thomas Cromwell for here, as this created such a great asset for future research.

In 1538-39, the Second Suppression of Religious Houses

Act or the Act for the Dissolution of the Greater Monasteries was passed through Parliament. This paved the way for the dissolution of the larger monasteries and other major religious houses. An additional five hundred institutions now all fell within scope of the wholesale liquidation and surrender of their land and assets to the crown.

The impact of the Dissolution on York was particularly severe. In November 1538, the Gilbertine priory of St Andrew's, which had previously been reprieved from closure by Robert Holgate's intervention, was forced to surrender.

The Augustinian friary on Lendal, the Franciscan Grey friary next to Castlegate, the Dominican Black friary in North Street and the Carmelite White friary off Fossgate all soon followed. In addition, Holy Trinity and St Clement's, both reopened during the Pilgrimage of Grace, were closed down for the second and final time.

The Act for the Dissolution of the Greater Monasteries meant even York's mightiest religious institutions discovered they were within scope of Cromwell's plans. As the diocese cathedral, only York Minster was spared. In November 1539, St Mary's Abbey was closed. During December, the last major religious house remaining in York, St Leonard's Hospital, was also surrendered. The assets of each of these long-standing religious institutions were transferred to the crown.

All the members of the religious orders who'd operated and lived in York's religious houses were effectively made unemployed and homeless. In York, in excess of sixty monks, sixty friars, twelve brothers, four canons, four sisters and ten nuns were affected. In addition to these, there were numerous novices, servants and others who'd worked in or supported the houses. Some, though by all means not all, of the ecclesiastical staff were fortunate enough to receive pensions, but this clearly wasn't the case for the ordinary citizens of York who also lost their livelihoods.

A number of the monks and canons did manage to secure roles elsewhere. Some amongst their number found positions not too far from their former homes, but others were forced to move much further afield. The last prior at St Mary's Abbey's for example accepted an appointment in a rectory in Norfolk, while several of York's monks became vicars or priests in local parish churches dotted around Yorkshire. A few even joined the parish clergy within the city walls.

The premises they had once lived in suffered various fates. St Mary's Abbey was retained by the crown, although most of the buildings, walls and structures were allowed to fall into disrepair or dismantled by the locals for building material. The notable exception to this was the abbot's house, which was retained by the crown for royal use in York.

Some of the sites, including Holy Trinity as previously described, were leased out. Others, including St Leonard's, were sold off. For example, St Andrew's was rented by and eventually bought outright by a future York alderman Richard Goldthorpe. He also purchased St Clement's.

Not a man to be left out when there was money to be made, Sir George Lawson took out a lease on the Augustinian house on Lendal, which was near to his home. When formal ownership of the plot of land was later granted outright to his family, the Lawsons converted the former friary into a malthouse and began to use it for brewing.

Many of the other monastic buildings and friaries were dismantled and the stone removed from them and used for building materials. Once closed, the houses no longer provided demand for goods from York's merchants or labour from York's workers. Merchants, tradesmen, labourers and others were badly hit. Butchers and wax chandlers, for example, saw sales of their meat and beeswax products much reduced, as they were no longer needed to feed or light the religious houses. Many other trades and guilds were similarly affected.

When St Leonard's Hospital was closed, no replacement institution was provided to support the poor, the ill or the destitute. The Dissolution also had a similarly detrimental impact on education in the city. In addition to providing care, St Leonard's had previously housed a school. This too was now closed. A number of poorer pupils had previously been housed and fed in St Mary's Abbey. This facility and the support it offered was also lost.

Ownership of between twenty and thirty percent of the city's housing stock, which had previously been controlled by York's resident and other religious houses across the country, transferred to the King. Henry's advisers sold many of these houses off. One London alderman, Sir Richard Gresham, alone purchased more than four hundred houses in York.

The major flow of money and wealth from the city was an economic disaster for York, particularly as it coincided with a severe and sustained outbreak of plague. Between the years of 1538 and 1541, York's population suffered above average death rates. It must have been a desperate time for many in the city.

In addition, following the Pilgrimage of Grace, Henry VIII was determined to keep a closer eye on York, Yorkshire in general and the other potentially rebellious counties of Northern England. In 1538, King Henry reinvigorated the Council of the North. The Council would now meet in four annual sessions with the former Gilbertine Master Robert Holgate as its new Lord President.

Once a year, the Council would hold session in each of Durham, Hull, Newcastle and York. When in York, the Council would reside in the old abbot's house of what until recently had been St Mary's Abbey. This building, which we now know as the King's Manor, was formally allocated to the Council of the

North in 1539.

Back in London, things had begun to go awry for the architect of the Dissolution, Thomas Cromwell. Just like his mentor Thomas Wolsey before him, Cromwell had enemies. They now conspired to convince the King that Cromwell was to blame for Henry's short-lived and ill-conceived marriage to his fourth wife Anne of Cleves.

Thomas Cromwell was arrested in 1540 and imprisoned in the Tower of London. He was beheaded on the very same day that Henry married his fifth wife Catherine Howard. What might this mean for York?

CHAPTER NINE
Henry VIII Comes to York

In addition to reinstating the Council of the North, Henry VIII wanted to demonstrate his personal power over the North and over York in particular. In September 1541, he made his one and only visit to the city during what became known as the King's Northern Progress. While in York, Henry also planned to hold talks with his nephew King James V of Scotland.

Prior to the King's arrival in York, the Corporation's leaders wanted to discover what they might be able to do to placate the royal anger which they were fully expecting to be vented on the city. They made requests to both Archbishop Lee and the Duke of Norfolk to advise them on what they should say to the King and what presents they should give him. York's aldermen also looked into what the city of Lincoln (which had had its own links with rebels) had done to submit to the King's majesty during his journey north. Meticulous plans and preparations were put into place in an attempt to ensure the city could restate its loyalty to the crown and get off as lightly as possible for its support for the Pilgrimage of Grace.

By custom, visiting monarchs entered York through Micklegate Bar on the western side of the city centre, just as Henry VII had done on several occasions. Plans and preparations were put in place to welcome Henry VIII along this route. However, this King had no wish to follow tradition.

On 18 September 1541, Henry arrived outside York with his much younger wife Catherine Howard and an armed force of five thousand horsemen and soldiers. They were followed by a mile long retinue of carriages, wagons, servants, cooks and supporting tradespeople. The events of the following days form the backdrop of C J Sansom's excellent novel *"Sovereign"* which I'd highly recommend as a very good read.

Henry had already been to Hull and was approaching York from the southeast side of the city rather than from the west. River crossings were difficult to come by and the King had no wish to make a detour to Micklegate. Instead, he arrived at the city's boundary at Fulford Cross on the southern edge of York.

Henry was met there by the Lord Mayor Robert Hall, the city's aldermen, numerous councillors and other local dignitaries. As the King approached them, York's leaders sank as one to their knees. In a prepared action, the city's recorder read out a lengthy statement, in which he apologised profusely on behalf of the people of York for the city's role during the Pilgrimage of Grace.

The recorder's speech included a frank admission of guilt: *"We your humble subjects the mayor, aldermen and commons of your grace's city of York and the inhabitants of your grace's county of your said city of York... have against our natural allegiance, disobediently and contrary to your grace's laws for the commonwealth provided, grievously, heinously and traitorously offended your high, invincible and most royal majesty your imperial crown and dignity in the most odious offence of traitorous rebellion."*

The recorder continued; having seen the error of their ways, York's leaders and its people were: *"...from the bottoms of our stomach repentant, woe and sorrowful for our said unnatural and heinous offences."*

In future, they would: *"... not only serve, obey, love and dread your royal majesty, spend our goods, our bodies without murmur or grudge in the service of your most royal majesty at your most gracious precepts and commandments utter affection of our heart's blood, but also we, our wives and children, continually devoutly pray to the most blessed and holy Trinity preserve your most royal majesty with your gracious queen, noble Prince Edward long to reign over us in prosperity..."*

When the full grovelling statement was finally over with, the local dignitaries showered the royal couple with gifts. The King and Queen were both presented with handsome silver cups which were filled to the brim with large quantities of gold. Suitably flattered and reassured, King Henry agreed to consider blessing the city with his forgiveness.

The King, Queen Catherine, their entourage and the York officials began to make their way towards the city walls. When the royal procession reached the gates and walls at Walmgate Bar, they were greeted there by York's main population.

During their time in York, Henry and Catherine stayed at the King's Manor. Other members of the royal party and various senior officials were given the best lodgings the city could find for them. Of course, most of the soldiers and servants camped out wherever they could find sufficient space. It isn't recorded if Henry, like Robert Aske, stopped the majority of his men from entering the city or made orders that all goods were to be paid for. For York's local population, it must have felt at times like their city was under occupation.

As previously discussed, royal visits were notoriously expensive. Despite the economic woes and hardships facing their city, the leaders of the Corporation of York had little choice but to host lavish feasts and celebrations for the King. Although they'd done the same for his father, this time the circumstances were quite different. During one of his visits, Henry VII had knighted Lord Mayor Todd and Alderman York for the city's loyalty to the crown and for holding out against an armed rebellion. This time, York had welcomed the rebels in. At the various banquets and entertainment, Lord Mayor Hall and the aldermen must have been feeling quite nervous.

Henry VIII, Queen Catherine and the King's army remained in York for nine long days. They left on 27 September. By this time, it was clear that the Scottish King James V had stood his uncle Henry up and wasn't coming to York. The reasons for this have long been debated over by historians. James may have been too ill to travel, or he may have wished to sleight Henry due to Scotland's alliance with France. Whatever his motives were, England and Scotland soon found themselves once again in armed conflict.

The Northern Progress withdrew from the city and after a second visit to Hull, Henry travelled south. The King's time in York must have been an uncomfortable period for the local population. Fortunately, there were no major disturbances, riots or unrest which needed to be put down by the royal army. While some traders no doubt did well from the visit, it's likely the sheer number and influx of people meant that the city was cleared of much of its food and a very large mess of detritus and waste was left behind. Of course, no-one was going to complain to the King.

During her brief visit to York, the Queen didn't know it, but she was living on borrowed time. Following the royal party's return south, she was accused of adultery, including incidents which were alleged to have taken place during the Northern Progress at Pontefract Castle. Catherine Howard was beheaded at the Tower of London in February 1542.

Henry VIII's Northern Progress was the last visit of any Tudor monarch to York. None of Henry's children, Mary, Elizabeth nor Edward, could be sufficiently bothered to make the journey north all the way from London. But at least the Corporation would save themselves the enormous expenditure which came with royal visits.

The next monarch to set foot in York would be the future Scots King James VI on his journey south from Edinburgh towards London in 1603 to be crowned James I of England. This would follow the death of Elizabeth I which would bring the Tudor era to an end.

But that was six decades off into the future. In 1543, Henry VIII married his sixth and final wife Catherine Parr. Although Catherine was a Protestant sympathiser, following the execution of Thomas Cromwell the slow Reformation of the Church in England had stalled. The Church's re-adoption of a more Catholic stance in religious matters was welcomed in York.

When the Archbishop of York Edward Lee died, he was replaced in 1545 by the Lord President of the Council of the North, Robert Holgate. One of Holgate's first acts was to create a plan to open a new grammar school in the city located next to York Minster. The current version of this school, Archbishop Holgate's, bears his name. However, these days it's located outside the city walls on the Hull Road.

Although many in York would have thought it was good to have a new grammar school and one so strongly supported by the Church, the Corporation's money worries continued. So did the King's needs for funds. Wars and Henry's extravagant expenditure were a constant drain on the government's coffers. Once again, the King and his advisors turned towards the Church for a source of funds. With the dissolution of the larger and lesser religious houses almost complete, even the smallest religious institution now came into view.

The first of the Chantries Acts was passed in 1545. This authorised a thorough review of the country's chantries. The various institutions within scope of this act included dedicated chapels in parts of larger churches and on private land, colleges, hospitals, free chapels, religious guilds and stipendiary services. The assets of any such body determined to be poorly governed or having other issues would be stripped away from them and passed to the crown.

With the sheer number of chantries in the city, York's leaders were rightfully concerned about what may happen next. However, the immediate impact on York and elsewhere was limited. Even though some investigations did begin, the commissioners lacked the rigour, vigour and leadership of Thomas Cromwell. Progress was slow. Little had been done and even less revenue raised from the chantries before Henry VIII's eventual death in January 1547.

The final years of Henry's reign had often been a difficult time for York. Wealth and employment had continued to fall. Major religious houses, hospitals and schools had closed. Healthcare, education and other services were increasingly hard to come by. What new hope and thinking might a new monarch bring?

CHAPTER TEN
Edward VI - Closure of York's Chantries and Religious Guilds

Henry VIII was succeeded by the male heir he'd longed for. However, there was still a problem. When Edward VI was crowned the new King of England in a lavish ceremony in Westminster Abbey in February 1547, he was just nine years old. Foreseeing the issues which might arise due to the age of his son, Henry left instructions that a Regency Council was to be put in place following his death. England would be ruled by this Council until the boy came of age. It was decided that the Council should be led by Edward's uncle, the Duke of Somerset Edward Seymour, who would now be known as the Lord Protector of the Realm.

Lord Protector Somerset faced similar challenges to those which had been encountered during the reign of Henry VIII. Conflict continued with Scotland and France and money was urgently needed to fill large holes in the country's ailing finances. Yet again, England's leaders turned their envious eyes towards the Church.

In 1547, Parliament passed the second Chantries Act. This strengthened and accelerated Henry's previous plans to get the crown's hands on the assets of the minor religious houses and other establishments. Commissioners were despatched up and down the country to urgently assess, close and liquidise the chantries and related religious buildings and institutions. All of their land and valuables were to be confiscated and the proceeds once again injected into the royal coffers.

The dissolution of the chantries is sometimes overlooked due to the greater emphasis placed on the surrender of the larger religious houses. However, the impact on York should not be underestimated. Although the smaller religious houses in the city hadn't completely filled the gap which had been left by the closure of institutions such as St Mary's Abbey and St Leonard's, they still provided charity and welfare to York's least fortunate citizens. When these houses were closed, their services ceased.

In York, the second Chantries Act led to the surrender to the crown of more than one hundred chantries, colleges and religious guilds. Many of the chantries consisted of relatively small, dedicated chapels which had been located within larger parish churches, including a number related to York Minster, and on private land. Another group of the clergy now became unemployed. Additionally, the goods and services which were previously purchased to support the chantries were no longed needed, leading to a further reduction in demand for York's merchants and tradesmen.

In addition to the trade guilds established by merchants and tradespeople, guilds could also be created for wider social or religious purposes. The 1547 Chantries Act impacted two important and relatively wealthy religious guilds in York. The first of these was the Corpus Christi guild.

Originally founded in 1408 to celebrate the Feast of Corpus Christi, the Corpus Christi guild had many members from within the upper reaches of the Church and from regional society, plus strong links to the Corporation of York. Richard III had even been a member.

From 1431 onwards, Corpus Christi was based at the chapel of St William on the Micklegate side of Ouse Bridge. If you are thinking of visiting, unfortunately there isn't a chapel there these days. Sadly, St William's was demolished in 1810 when a replacement bridge was built, although it can be still seen in a number of paintings of Ouse Bridge which date back to the beginning of the nineteenth century or earlier. In addition, a series of illustrations were made of the chapel before its demolition. These are now available to view in York City Art Gallery.

The guild was closely connected to the annual Corpus Christi celebrations and processions held in York, although the origin of these pre-dates the establishment of the guild itself. The procession followed the traditional route the King (barring Henry VIII, of course) took when visiting York, starting in Micklegate, crossing over Ouse Bridge, progressing through Coney Street and along Stonegate before reaching York Minster. The Corpus Christi or Mystery Plays were organised by the Corporation of York in collaboration with various guilds in the city.

More importantly for the new King and the Regency Council, the Corpus Christi guild in York with its wealthy membership base was asset rich. Its gold and silver shrine alone was valued at over £200. The shrine and the guild's other disposable assets were quickly confiscated by the crown.

The second wealthy religious guild in York at the beginning of King Edwards's reign was the Guild of St Christopher and St George. This was located at St George's Chapel, near to York Castle. When the guild was closed and its assets seized, the Corporation of York at least managed to purchase its land and buildings.

During the reign of Elizabeth I, St George's was used as a house of correction, providing forced labour and housing for paupers who'd previously refused to work. Sadly, this building also no longer exists. However, these days (at least when it's not flooded) it's possible to park your car there on the St George's Field car park.

In addition, the ownership of another five hundred domestic houses in York which had previously belonged to the chantries and related institutions passed over to the crown. Many of these properties were auctioned off in the coming months to the highest bidder. Once again, funds and wealth were flying out of York.

Despite the protection offered by Archbishop Holgate, not even York Minster could fully escape the effects of what was going on. A number of chantries located in the Minster were closed down, their assets confiscated and handed over to the crown. In October 1547, the Privy Council also demanded the Archbishop surrender a significant amount of additional silver which had been held in the Minster.

By now a sizeable fortune had left the jurisdiction of the Church in York. When the last treasurer of the Minster resigned from his position, his house and assets in the Minster Yard were seized by the crown. As previously mentioned, the Treasurer's House these days is open to visitors. If you're in York, you should pop in. It's a very interesting National Trust property.

In 1547, King Edward presented the Treasurer's House as a gift to his uncle Lord Protector Somerset. A year later, Archbishop Holgate, by now a wealthy man in his own right, bought the house from Somerset. Having previously stayed in official residences at the King's Manor as Lord President of the Council of the North and at the Church's palace in Bishopthorpe, perhaps Robert Holgate felt he needed a private property he could call his own.

CHAPTER ELEVEN
Reformation and Plague

King Edward VI and Lord Protector Seymour were Protestants. Under their leadership, the Church and parts of the country had begun to move in a Protestant direction. Whether swaying along with the prevailing political winds or due to his own evolving religious beliefs, Archbishop Holgate began to support the move away from Catholicism. Although the subtle changes he made were felt most where he had direct control, for example at York Minster, one of the more interesting actions Holgate took was made possible by a change in the law which allowed clergymen to marry.

Although by the time of King Edward, Archbishop Holgate was in his sixties, the woman he planned to wed Barbara Wentworth was around twenty-five years old. More controversially it was claimed Barbara already had a husband, as she'd been married in a church in front of witnesses. We covered her wedding briefly in an earlier chapter. It had taken place two decades previously, when Barbara had been only five years old and the alderman's son she *"married"* was just seven.

Since reaching adulthood, Barbara had consistently refused to recognise the wedding. In 1549, she took legal action in an attempt to get the marriage annulled. Details of the court's ruling are not available, but the result must have fallen in her favour. In January 1550, Barbara Wentworth and Robert Holgate were married in Bishopthorpe. We'll return to review the implications of the Holgates' union shortly.

Despite his youth, Edward VI was an ardent Protestant. Supported by the King and the Lord Protector, the Archbishop of Canterbury Thomas Cranmer began to push through a series of religious reforms to the Church in England. These made it much more Protestant in nature than it had been before under the King's father Henry VIII.

The 1549 Act of Uniformity declared the contents of the 1549 Book of Common Prayer would be used as the one and only legal form of religious worship in England. The new prayer book was written in English rather than in Latin. Communion, Matins and Evensong services would all now be conducted in the English language. Importantly for Robert Holgate, as mentioned above the law was also changed to give permission for clergymen to marry.

The new laws were highly controversial. The governing classes and the country in general were split down the middle. Ten bishops voted in favour of the Act of Uniformity, while eight bishops voted against. Catholics, including those in more religiously conservative areas such as Yorkshire, criticised the changes for containing too many Protestant elements. Protestants argued the reforms weren't radical enough and far too much Catholic doctrine had been retained.

When the new act became law, a much larger number of Catholic practices were banned than had been the case under Thomas Cromwell. The changes included major alterations to the interior of each parish church. Altars, rood screens and many other fixtures and fittings were scheduled to be removed. A much more austere form of worship was called for and orders given that many of the more ornate decorations should be taken down or painted over.

In York, the changes were often met with resistance. In a number of churches, the altars had to be forcibly removed. When some of the valuables in the parish churches were due to be confiscated, this was sometimes avoided in the city by the priest or his parishioners hiding them and storing them away, in the hope of better (more Catholic) times in future. Like their Archbishop, York's clergymen were also given the option to marry, although only a fairly small number of them are known to have taken advantage of this.

Unlike during the Pilgrimage of Grace, there's no evidence of a large-scale local uprising against the changes being enforced on the city. Nor is there significant evidence of the prosecution of individuals for failing to comply with government directives, although one man, Thomas Vavasour a medical doctor who we'll focus on later, was temporarily forced to leave the city.

In parallel to the closure of the chantries and the religious guilds, the changes made to religious services and the stripping of church fittings, a further bill was put through Parliament which would impact York's parishes and churches. However, this change was directly requested by the Corporation of York rather than anyone else and it provided no revenue or any other direct benefit to the crown.

With the city's population still in decline, the Corporation's leaders believed York simply possessed too many churches for a city of its size. The 1547 Act for the Uniting of Certain Churches in the City of York acknowledged this, as being part and parcel of the *"ruin and decay of the said city"*. The act explicitly gave York's mayor and aldermen the permission to *"unite and knit together the said parishes into a fewer number"* and *"pull down the churches they think superfluous"*.

By 1547, York still had thirty-eight parish churches. Of these, around a dozen were identified as being prime candidates for either merger or closure. Although the plan wasn't fully completed in the short term, between 1549 and 1550 six of these churches were sold off to members of the Corporation at bargain prices. It appears it wasn't just Members of Parliament who were out to make a profit.

Although there were no major uprisings in York at this time, this wasn't the case across the whole of the country. Partly fuelled by unrest in rural areas due to the illegal enclosures of common land, popular uprisings took place in Norfolk, the West Country and elsewhere. Although the rebellions were eventually put down, the impact on the Lord Protector's reputation was significant. Edward Seymour was arrested in 1549 and executed in 1552. The new de facto leader of the country until Edward came of age was John Dudley, the Earl of Warwick and Duke of Northumberland. Dudley decided to adopt the title of Lord President Northumberland.

A second Act of Uniformity was passed. This introduced further Protestant reforms and removed some of the remaining traces of Catholicism from the Church in England. Attendance of the official church service became mandatory. Any clergy or lay people found guilty of non-attendance could be fined or imprisoned.

Meanwhile, the people of York had more immediate concerns. The city was struck down by a series of epidemics, including bubonic plague and sweating sickness. In the years 1550 and 1551, York's parish registers regularly listed particularly high rates of burials and mortality. In some places, the impact was even more devastating. For example, the parish of St Martin's in Micklegate may have lost up to half of its population.

The situation was further exacerbated by poor weather. In 1551, the city was hit by a great storm. The winds were so severe they brought down the steeples of multiple churches, including those above Trinity Church on Micklegate and the Church of St John's.

On top of all this, the surrounding countryside experienced a number of failed harvests. During the winter months in particular, there were cases of malnutrition in some of the poorer quarters of the city. With epidemics and famine combining, the death rate remained high both throughout the winter and summer seasons. It was around this time or shortly afterwards during the reign of Queen Mary that York's dwindling population reached its low point of less than eight thousand people.

CHAPTER TWELVE
Mary I - Return of the Catholic Church

After several months of illness, Edward VI died at Greenwich Palace in July 1553. At the time of his death, he was just fifteen years old. Suspecting the King's condition would become terminal, a plan of succession was put into place with the primary aim of preventing the restoration of the Catholic Church in England. Crucially, this plan excluded the King's Catholic half-sister Mary from becoming Queen. More surprisingly it also prevented Edward's Protestant half-sibling Elizabeth from taking the crown.

Instead, the previous leader of the Regency Council, the Duke of Northumberland, supported by the Privy Council, announced Edward's chosen heir was the King's cousin Lady Jane Grey. Perhaps it was merely coincidence that Jane happened to be Northumberland's daughter-in-law. When this announcement was made it was met with derision and anger. Following Edward's death, a power struggle ensued. It didn't last very long. The culmination was the arrest and execution of Lady Jane Grey, her father-in-law the Duke of Northumberland and several others.

One of the many men arrested in the aftermath was Henry Hastings, the son and heir of the Earl of Huntingdon. Although Hastings had supported Northumberland's plans, upon his release from prison he swore his loyalty to Mary. This was despite her Catholicism and his own Puritanical leanings. Hastings will come back into the book later as one of the most important Lord Presidents of the Council of the North.

On 1 October 1553, Edward's elder half-sister Mary, the devoutly Catholic daughter of Henry VIII and his first wife Catherine of Aragon, was crowned as Queen Mary I of England in Westminster Abbey. The new Queen and her supporters quickly acted to restore Catholicism as the state religion of England.

In September 1553, Catholic Mass was reintroduced into the country's church services. Over the coming months, many of the Parliamentary acts relating to religion which had been passed during the reigns of Mary's father Henry and her half-brother Edward were repealed.

The changes made to the law also acknowledged the Pope rather than the country's monarch was the sole head of the Church in England. This allowed the country to reconcile with the Catholic Church in Rome. In 1554, hoping to ensure a Catholic succession to the throne, Mary married King Philip II of Spain. The Reformation of the Church in England appeared to be over.

In religiously conservative York, Mary's accession to the throne and the actions she was taking (with the significant exception of her marriage to the Spanish King) were largely welcomed. After her coronation, the Corporation of York issued a letter which pledged the city's allegiance to the new monarch. The letter praised Mary for being, "*so noble, Godly and most rightful a Queen*".

Many of York's parish churches were gradually repaired and restored. The altars and other fittings which had been forcibly removed during Edward's reign were replaced, although this was sometimes a slow process. Many of the refurbishments which were needed could only take place when the individual parishes and some of their wealthier parishioners had sufficient funds to pay for them.

A fascinating example of the restoration of a parish church in York to return it to its previous Catholic glory took place at St Martin's in Coney Street. In 1555, the father of Saint Margaret Clitherow, Thomas Middleton, began his three-year term as a churchwarden there. Thomas and his three fellow churchwardens set about completing the refurbishment of the church in time for the Easter services.

The churchwardens' tasks included re-establishing the rood crucifix, which was sited between the chancel and the nave of the church, and the rood screen beneath it. New candlesticks were bought to illuminate the rood. Repairs were made to the Easter Sepulchre, the arched recess where the crucifix and other sacred pieces relating to the resurrection were displayed between Good Friday and Easter Sunday.

Thomas Middleton and his colleagues organised the purchase and fitting of new materials for the altar cloth and bought a new supply of charcoal for the Easter vigil service. Finally, they funded the work which was needed to repair several of the damaged stalls which were used to house the choir and congregation. Similar work was taking place in many of York's other parish churches.

One striking aspect of the return to Catholicism was the state persecution of leading Protestants. Nearly three hundred people were executed in England and Wales during Mary's relatively short reign for their religious beliefs, including in excess of fifty women. Many of them suffered the horrific death of being burned at the stake. This earned the Queen the infamous nickname and title of Bloody Mary.

A number of prominent Protestant bishops, including the Archbishop of Canterbury Thomas Cranmer, were amongst those to be executed. Hundreds of other leading Protestants fled to the continent to escape persecution and possible death. Amongst their number were three future Archbishops of York, Thomas

Young, Edmund Grindal and Edwin Sandys.

In October 1553, the then Archbishop of York Robert Holgate was arrested. Holgate was accused of committing *"diverse"* offences and imprisoned in the Tower of London. At least one of the accusations against him was related to his marriage to Barbara Wentworth. Under Catholic law, clergymen weren't given permission to marry.

While in prison, Holgate was stripped of his position as the Archbishop of York. In response, the former archbishop denounced his marriage. He claimed he'd only agreed to get married *"unwisely"* and under considerable pressure which had been placed upon him by the previous regime.

Unlike many of the other Protestant bishops, Robert Holgate wasn't executed. Having rejected his marriage, he went on to renounce the Protestant faith. In January 1555, Holgate was released from prison and instructed to live a quiet life. He died away from the public eye only ten months later.

You may be wondering (like me) about the fate of his wife Barbara Holgate (née Wentworth). Sadly, no definitive records have been found which fully explain what happened to Barbara following her husband's arrest, his rejection of their marriage and subsequent release from gaol. An unsubstantiated report written some time later claims by this time the couple had two children. The same report asserts that Barbara also returned to live with Anthony Norman, the man who'd previously claimed to be her husband following their childhood betrothal. To date, no definitive proof has yet been discovered to show if this was true. It may have been the case. We just don't know.

In 1555, Nicholas Heath was appointed as the new Archbishop of York to replace Robert Holgate. Although he didn't know it at the time, Heath would be the last Catholic to serve in the post. Having also been appointed as the Queen's Lord Chancellor, Archbishop Heath was forced to spend less time in York than his predecessor.

However, he did make a difference. In contrast to many other cities in England, London in particular, there wasn't a single prosecution or execution of a Protestant for religious heresy in York during the whole of Queen Mary's reign. This may have been partly due to York having been a religiously traditionalist city, but there would have been Protestants there. It appears likely that another reason for the absence of any executions was down to Archbishop Heath's efforts. They may not have realised it, but York's citizens had much to thank their absent Archbishop for.

CHAPTER THIRTEEN
The Russians are Coming

Of course, life in York under Queen Mary wasn't all about religion. Ordinary people went about their daily lives. Some of the wealthier men and merchants were elected as sheriffs and aldermen. Some would go on to serve the city as Lord Mayor. The following men were Lord Mayors of York during Queen Mary's reign, William Cowpland, John North, William Beckwith, Richard Goldthorpe, Robert Hall and finally Ralph Hall. All of them apart from Beckwith also served as a Member of Parliament for York at one time or another. Interestingly though, not one of the six Lord Mayors who succeeded them was elected as an MP during the reign of Queen Elizabeth.

Although Queen Mary didn't visit York, a record was made of another interesting visitor to the city during her reign. The fascinating book *The Antiquities of York City, and the Civil Government Thereof... Collected from the Papers of Christopher Halyard* was published in the eighteenth century. The contents include a detailed list of the names of the mayors, sheriffs and other Corporation officials appointed in the years between 1273 and 1719.

The book also contains various snippets of fascinating information. These include an intriguing one-liner dated as having taken place in 1557. This was during the second mayoral term of Robert Hall. The brief and succinct entry states: *"This year the King of Muscovie came to York"*.

The ruler of Moscow at this time was the first Tsar of

Russia, Ivan the Terrible. As far as we know (and it's very likely we would have known if he had) Ivan the Terrible never visited England. Why then was this claim made?

There's one possible and perhaps even likely explanation. During the years 1556 and 1557, Russia sent its first official envoy to England. The journey of Osip Nepeya to the country is considered by many to be the first instance of any formal diplomatic relations between Russia and England. This is interesting, but did Envoy Nepeya ever travel to York? If he did, it was probably his own visit to the city the cryptic entry refers to.

At the very least, Nepeya's story is a fascinating one. He set off from Russia in August 1556 in a convoy of four ships. Two of the four were destroyed in a great storm in the North Sea between Norway and Scotland. The third managed to make it to port in Trondheim. The fourth was carried off course by the storm until it reached the east coast of Scotland where it was wrecked on the coast and looted.

The envoy Osip Nepeya was one of a handful of survivors. After they'd made land, the men made their way to Edinburgh. Eventually in February 1557 they travelled south to London. It would be very likely they would have stayed in York during this journey, following the same route in reverse which had been travelled by Margaret Tudor in 1503. Even if this was the case, why do the records indicate York was visited by the *"King"* of Moscow rather than his envoy?

When Nepeya finally reached London, he was reported to be wearing a formal uniform. This included a *"long dress, red boots and a white cap"*. Upon his arrival in the city, he was greeted personally by Mary I accompanied by a large number of officials and merchants. A lavish ceremony was held to welcome the Russian delegation.

Nepeya's clothing and royal welcome were so grand, one

English merchant Henry Machynhe described him as the *"Duke of Muscovy"*. Perhaps the Corporation of York's officials, or the editor of the book Christopher Halyard, made the same mistake when Nepeya visited York?

Much of Nepeya's mission to England regarded negotiating new trade agreements and the opening up of trade routes between Russia and England. The envoy's appearance in York would certainly have invited the interest of members of the guild of the Mercers of the City of York (later known as the Merchant Adventurers) due to their desire to drive significant additional business with the Baltic states.

There's also an interesting report in the History of Parliament's entry for one of York's Members of Parliament, the alderman and twice Lord Mayor Robert Hall, the husband of Jane Hall. Jane, if you remember, was the daughter of William Harrington, the Lord Mayor at the time of the Pilgrimage of Grace and as such a relative of Guy Fawkes.

Are you following all this? Don't worry if you're not, and apologies for using so many names and connections, but it's interesting to see just how many of York's families at this time were in some way interlinked. Anyway, the report states that Robert Hall paid for the lodgings of a Russian ambassador at his own cost when he passed through York on his way to London. So, it looks like the entry did, after all, refer to the visit of the Russian envoy Osip Nepeya, rather than anyone else. It was certainly not Ivan the Terrible.

Ambassador Nepeya's visit to England also included a second link to Yorkshire. The Russian envoy is reported to have *"witnessed"* a failed uprising in April 1557. This was when the exiled noble Thomas Stafford landed with two ships and a group of armed men at Scarborough on the Yorkshire coast. Stafford's force soon took control of Scarborough Castle. Their intention was to raise a nationwide uprising against Queen Mary due to her unpopular marriage with Philip II of Spain.

However, Stafford and the rebels were soon arrested. One report indicates that York's Lord Mayor Robert Hall played an active part in their downfall, so it's possible Envoy Nepeya did directly witness what happened while he was in Yorkshire. After being imprisoned in the Tower of London, the rebels were tried and found guilty of treason. In the aftermath, Stafford and thirty of his followers were executed.

Perhaps Osip Nepeya shared the story of the English rebels' arrest and grisly fate with Tsar Ivan when he returned to Moscow. Certainly, from the time of Nepeya's return to Russia onwards, the Tsar's domestic policies changed quite dramatically from focusing on relatively peaceful reforms to bloody persecution and largescale executions of rebels, both real and suspected.

CHAPTER FOURTEEN
Inflation and the New Ague

Improved trade links with countries like Russia would certainly have been a major benefit to York's ailing economy. We'll return to this subject later. During the 1550's however, York was still suffering from economic hardship.

During much of Queen Mary's reign, the city like the whole of England was experiencing a bout of inflation and rising prices. In 1555-56, the Lord Mayor of York, a merchant called William Beckwith, wrote to the city's Members of Parliament to inform them just how difficult it was to collect taxes in the city due to the abject poverty being felt in some of York's least wealthy parishes.

Beckwith wrote: *"It would have pitied a man's heart to see what hard shift many a poor man and woman made, for some were fain to sell their pot or their pan and other implements, some laid their apparel to pledge to pay with their tax; and of certain vacant houses in the decayed parishes the collectors had nothing to distrain but took off the doors and windows to make up stake with."*

This obviously was a dire time for many people. At least Lord Mayor Beckwith appeared to be displaying some true concern for the straits that York's citizens often found themselves in. One of his responsibilities as mayor was to act as a clerk for the city's markets. In the extreme, this gave the Lord Mayor the power to set prices and ensure they were being observed by traders in York.

In 1555, Beckwith did just this. Lord Mayor Beckwith *"went through the market to see reasonable prices of visuals"*. During his rounds, he was shocked to see the prices being changed by some of the butchers who he considered were *"selling flesh excessively"*. The Lord Mayor decided to take firm action and instructed the men to reduce their meat prices to levels which were much more *"reasonable for the poor"*.

Seeing such an obvious level of deprivation in their city, York's leaders decided to take some action to improve the provision of education and healthcare. With Archbishop Holgate's grammar school now in place, the Dean and Chapter of York Minster planned to create a second more distinctly Catholic grammar school *"for education and instruction of a certain number of scholars and the maintenance of a schoolmaster"*.

These days the modern version of the school is located on the street of Bootham. St Peter's is reported to have been founded by St Paulinus of York in 627 A.D. at the site occupied today by York Minster. This would make it one of the oldest schools in the world. However, by the time of Queen Mary's reign St Peter's had been dormant for some time.

When the school was re-established by the Church in the sixteenth century, St Peter's was initially known locally as the Free School. The reformed school was positioned just outside the city walls near to the Horse Fair at the intersection of Gillygate and Lord Mayor's Walk. The site of the school had previously been used to house a number of minor religious buildings, including St Anne's Chapel. Today, you'll find the Union Terrace car park there. Perhaps one day, as in Leicester, there'll be an excavation. Who knows what they might find underneath?

While the Church had placed some of its focus on improving education in the city, the Corporation of York recognised the dire need to improve healthcare facilities following the huge gaps left open two decades earlier by the dissolution of the religious houses. As a result, the Corporation wrote a letter to the newly appointed Archbishop of Canterbury Cardinal Reginald Pole requesting him to approve and fund the restoration of St Leonard's Hospital.

Although the Corporation didn't secure a positive reply to this letter, they did receive good news elsewhere on the financial front. Queen Mary decided to approve a series of tax rebates which she hoped would address, partially at least, the *"great ruin and poverty"* being felt in York.

The crown also returned to the Corporation some of the incomes which had been lost from the chantries and related institutions when they'd been removed from local control during King Edward's reign. The Corporation received a significant sum from this change, equivalent to an additional £157 of revenue per annum. The proceeds from these changes must have been gratefully received by the aldermen and their fellow councillors. Let's hope they spent it wisely on addressing the needs of their citizens, particularly those in abject poverty.

During the latter years of Queen Mary's reign, York would have found good use for a hospital like St Leonard's. Sadly, the city was struck down once more by pestilence. These days the *"new ague"* is believed to have been a particularly virulent strain of influenza. In 1558, the disease spread rapidly across the country, very much like a Tudor version of Covid-19. York, like many other places, was severely impacted. Burial rates across many of the city's parishes were once again very high.

In the final months of 1558, news reached the North of England that the Catholic Queen was unwell. Although Mary had married King Philip II of Spain to ensure a Catholic succession, the couple remained childless. When the Queen became severely ill, she confirmed her half-sister Elizabeth, the daughter of Henry VIII and Anne Boleyn, should be her successor. Knowing Elizabeth had been raised as a Protestant must have been a bitter pill for the dying Catholic Queen Mary to swallow.

When Mary died in November 1558 possibly from cancer, she was just forty-two years old. Coincidentally, her Catholic Archbishop of Canterbury, Reginald Pole, died on the very same day. Like many others in York and beyond, Pole had fallen foul of a severe bout of influenza. With the Catholic Queen Mary about to be replaced by her Protestant half-sister, the outlook in York must have looked bleak indeed.

CHAPTER FIFTEEN
Elizabeth I - Supremacy and Uniformity

Elizabeth was crowned as the Queen of England in Westminster Abbey in January 1559. She was twenty-five years old. The country she was about to rule over was blighted by disease, had suffered from poor harvests and continued to wage war with its neighbours. York and the wider country were struggling, but change was on its way.

There's little doubt that the Corporation and the people of York in general greeted Elizabeth's accession to the throne with significantly less enthusiasm than they'd felt for her half-sister. What they couldn't know at the time was that their city was about to fare far better under Elizabeth than any of the other Tudor monarchs.

One of the most striking changes was the major reduction in the incidence of serious illness in the city. This began immediately. After the significant death tolls which had been suffered during the new ague influenza epidemic of 1558, there wasn't a single widespread outbreak of disease in York during the whole of the reign of Elizabeth I. Ironically, the next time a major epidemic would sweep through York would be in 1604 in the year following Elizabeth's death. At that time, the plague would return to the city in the early months of the reign of her cousin, the first Stuart sovereign of England, James I.

Early on during Elizabeth's own reign, Parliament passed two new Acts of Supremacy and Uniformity. The Supremacy Act confirmed Elizabeth, rather than the Pope, was the Supreme

Governor of the Church of England, while the Act of Uniformity was designed to establish a *"uniform order of Religion"* in England based upon the 1552 Book of Common Prayer. This had been created by Thomas Cranmer during Edward VI's reign. With the country moving once again in a Protestant direction, the Church of England broke away from Rome for a second and (to date) final time.

Regional commissions were set up to verify that the Acts of Supremacy and Uniformity were being properly implemented and enforced around the country. The commissions' new leaders were mostly senior Protestant clergymen, including some who'd only recently returned to England following their enforced exile on the continent to evade persecution and execution during the bloody reign of Queen Mary.

Any Catholic bishops who refused to swear the oath of royal supremacy were removed from office. However, they weren't executed or burned at the stake, as many of the leading Protestant bishops had suffered under the previous regime. Their senior roles in the Church were passed on to loyalist Protestants. For example, Elizabeth appointed her mother's former chaplain Matthew Parker as the new Archbishop of Canterbury, replacing the now deceased Catholic Cardinal Reginald Pole.

In York, the Archbishop Nicholas Heath was one of a number of the Catholic bishops who stated they remained loyal to the new Queen but, due to their Catholic beliefs, they could not support the wording of the Acts of Supremacy and Uniformity. For this reason, Heath was removed from his position as Archbishop of York, although he wasn't prosecuted. Instead, he was allowed to retire quietly from public life. A replacement Archbishop wouldn't be appointed for another two years.

Meanwhile, Parliamentary and ecclesiastical battles were being fought out about just how far and how fast the new religious changes could go. A series of compromises were made to retain some elements of Catholicism in the Church and church services. At times, this approach caused almost as many issues for the Protestant clergy as Catholics. For example, when Elizabeth attempted to permit rood crucifixes to be retained in the parish churches, many senior Protestant churchmen protested, including two future Archbishops of York, Edmund Grindal and Edwin Sandys. Knowing she could ill afford to lose her Protestant bishops as well as the Catholic ones, Elizabeth relented.

Some of the new commissioners would have liked to have gone even further than the new laws which changed and reformed the religious practices in the churches within their jurisdiction. Items considered to be idolatrous, including rood crucifixes and screens of the type so lovingly restored at St Martin's in Coney Street by Thomas Middleton, were often removed from their churches and burned. In certain parishes the altars, images and other pieces were removed and hidden away by the local priests or parishioners in the belief that one day they could be brought back when Catholicism returned, as had been the case during the transition from Edward to Mary.

The commissioners called together the senior clergy in every area to ensure their adherence to the royal supremacy, the prayer book and the changing laws. Despite some of the compromises being made, many clergymen refused to attend. Some were incensed by what they saw as nothing short of vandalism being carried out in their churches. As a punishment, the men who continued to dissent were removed from their parishes. In some areas, the dismissals, following the widespread outbreaks of influenza and other epidemics, resulted in an acute shortage of clergymen.

In 1561, Thomas Young was appointed as the new Archbishop of York. He'd previously been one of the leading

Protestant figures who'd been forced to flee from England to mainland Europe during the time of Queen Mary. Upon his return to the country, Young's loyalty and adherence to the Protestant faith had led to a rapid rise up the ranks of the Protestant clergy. Born in Pembrokeshire in Wales, he'd become the Bishop of St David's, before swiftly being promoted to the second most important position in the Church of England as the Archbishop of York.

The timing of Thomas Young's appointment was no coincidence. Around this time, the Ecclesiastical Commission for the Northern Province was being created by royal letters patent. Once established, this new commission was to be based in York and presided over by the Archbishop. The Ecclesiastical Commission quickly established itself as the second most important court in the whole of the north of England, second only to the Council of the North. Both played a major role in enforcing the religious uniformity laws, as demanded by the Queen and her Parliament.

Archbishop Young believed there was much work to be done in his diocese. In York, Young and his fellow commissioners quickly called together the district's senior clergymen. The group consisted of around ninety men. A mere twenty-one of them agreed to appear personally before the commissioners to subscribe to the new policies. Sixteen sent proxies as representatives in their place, while thirty-six men appeared but declined to subscribe to the new legislation. A further seventeen didn't even respond to the Commission's request.

Clearly a significant number of York's clergy wished to resist or attempt to ignore the new legislation. Some of these men, including Henry Moore, the rector of St Martin's in Micklegate, were forcibly removed from their parishes. This type of punishment, which also removed men from their homes and their livelihoods, often proved to be effective.

Several of York's previously Catholic clergy, including Henry Moore, relented. After they promised to conform, men like Moore were allowed to return to their churches. With a number of their fellow clergymen having died during the disease ridden 1550s, for a time the Church in York faced a struggle to retain sufficient clergymen to man the remaining parish churches. Sometimes one vicar was forced to administer several different parishes.

Archbishop Young and the new ecclesiastical commissioners soon took to their task. Additional Protestants were actively recruited to join the city's clergymen. A number of these men were given positions at York Minster. The pace of change in some of York's parish churches however was far slower. A few parishes, including Thomas Middleton's place of worship at St Martin's in Coney Street, actively resisted the removal of their altars and images by the commissioners. Others did what they were told, but only under duress and the threat of punishment. Some, as described above, did their best to hide many of the key items away to bring them back for another day. Unfortunately for them, that day wasn't to come.

CHAPTER SIXTEEN
The Great Flood

With the absence of any major illness or epidemic, York's parish registers finally began to record higher numbers of baptisms rather than burials during the 1560's. Immigration into the city, mainly from elsewhere in England, was also on the rise. To make up for the previous shortfalls in the local population, many of York's professional guilds had allowed tradesmen to take on apprentices from outside the city. Such men could eventually become freemen of York in their own right, usually by paying a set price. As the population grew in the 1560s, the practice became much less common. Later in the decade, the Corporation's Common Council introduced controls to prevent such *"strangers"* from being enfranchised for less than £10.

One of the factors which was driving the renewed growth in the city's wealth at this time was the establishment in York of the Ecclesiastical Commission for the Northern Province. The new commission brought professional men such as lawyers and court officials to the city, while its court hearings and sessions brought additional visitors. All needed somewhere to eat, to drink and to lodge, bringing valuable business to York's shops, markets, inns and alehouses.

The Council of the North too had a significant impact. In previous decades, the Council had sat in annual sessions in each of the cities of Durham, Hull, Newcastle and York. In 1561, the Council's constitution was changed. This followed a successful request from the Council's representatives to the national government. From then on, the Council was permanently located in York. Several leading councillors had argued that this would bring benefits to the city's ailing economy and enable the Council to reduce its running costs. Of course, it also made life significantly easier for many of the Council's officers. Travelling around the country in Tudor times was often neither convenient nor pleasant.

Just as the closure of the religious houses had caused money to flood out of York, the establishment of these two large regional administrative bodies resulted in wealth, employment and trade flowing back into the city. As York's finances improved, the Corporation began to make a number of civic improvements. These were certainly needed in 1564 when the bridge over the river Ouse was seriously damaged.

The *Antiquities of York* records the incident as follows: *"This year {1564} on twelfth-day, Ouse Bridge was broken down, by reason of a great snow and sudden thaw. The water did rise to a great height, in so much as the flood and ice being so vehement that two bows within one arch and twelve houses standing upon the bridge were overthrown, and twelve persons drowned".*

In addition to the loss of life and housing, the impact on the city was significant. Ouse Bridge was the only road crossing point over the main river which ran through the centre of the walled city. Rather like in 2015 in the nearby town of Tadcaster, Tudor York was temporarily split into two.

The Minster, York Castle, the Council of the North, the Corporation of York and the city's main shops and markets were all located on the north-eastern side of the river. A smaller but still significant part of the city's population was isolated and cut off from the city's amenities on the other side.

The main road into York from London, the Midlands, the south and the west of the country entered the city via Micklegate on the western side. This road was now effectively blocked. In Tudor times, bridges over major rivers like the Ouse were few and far between. A temporary ferry service was initiated. This enabled people and goods to cross the river in the centre of the city. If this was insufficient or the queue was too long, the only alternative was to make a lengthy diversion to cross the Ouse by ferry at another location such as at Naburn, four or five miles south of the city.

Repairs to the bridge to enable pedestrians, animals, carts, wagons and carriages to cross over was a major priority. The Corporation's bridgemasters were junior officers usually only responsible for collecting revenues such as bridge tolls and managing routine maintenance of the city's bridges. They now had to take on a task of major importance. The rebuilding of Ouse Bridge was one of the largest and most important engineering projects in the North of England at this time. It was also going to cost a lot of money.

The Corporation levied an additional local tax to raise funds to pay for the work. The money raised was supplemented by a series of donations made by wealthy merchants. The new bridge's design included the creation of a much larger single central arch span as a replacement for the destroyed segments. A number of buildings on the top of the bridge also needed to be replaced.

The repairs were completed sufficiently to allow people and goods to cross the river two years later in 1566. This was about a year after the death of Robert Hall, the former Lord Mayor of York who'd hosted the Russian envoy when he'd made his way through York. When Robert Hall died, he left money in his will to fund a selection of good causes, including help for the poor and the maintenance of York's highways.

When Hall's widow Jane died shortly afterwards, she carried on her husband's good work. The *Antiquities of York* book reports in *"This year {1566} was Ouse Bridge built up again; towards which good work the Lady Jane Hall widow, and relief of Robert Hall, late alderman deceased, gave by her will one hundred pounds"*.

A year afterwards, the river was dredged in a major effort to prevent any further reoccurrence of the issue. Following this, the riverbank was built up to protect the city from future deluges. Although York continues to be regularly affected by flooding to this day, the work was largely successful. The rebuilt bridge continued to provide a safe road crossing over the river Ouse until it was replaced by a new construction which was completed almost two hundred and fifty years later in 1821.

CHAPTER SEVENTEEN
Council v Corporation

Shortly before the collapse of Ouse Bridge, Archbishop Young had become an even busier man than usual. Like Archbishop Holgate before him, Thomas Young was appointed as the new Lord President of the Council of the North. In addition to being Archbishop of York and the leader of the Northern Ecclesiastical Commission, Archbishop Young was now responsible for the most important court of justice in the whole of the northern half of the country. The role included enforcing the Queen's laws across all of the North of England. By holding all three of the positions at once, Young was demonstrating the close ties and connections which existed between the English state and the Church during the reign of Elizabeth I.

By the time of Archbishop Young's appointment, the Council of the North had changed from holding sessions in several different cities across the north to being permanently headquartered in the King's Manor in York in the old abbot's house in the former grounds of St Mary's Abbey. One impact of the change was that the Lord President and his fellow Council members perhaps had more time to focus on events in York than they otherwise might have. The leaders of the Council certainly began to take a dim view of what they considered was happening, or not happening, across the city centre in the Corporation of York's offices at the Common Hall (now known as the Guildhall).

While members of the Council of the North were appointed

by the Queen or government officials, the officers of the Corporation of York were generally local men, locally appointed and locally elected. The highest levels of the Corporation were dominated by York's wealthiest merchants. Although the country may have flip-flopped between monarchs and religious directions, many of its people hadn't. This was certainly true in York where, as we've seen, priests and parishioners sometimes attempted to push back against the Protestant religious reforms being imposed upon them.

In the 1560's, many of the Corporation's councillors and aldermen retained a great deal of sympathy for and sometimes adherence to the Catholic Church. In 1564, the Council of the North raised a formal complaint against the Corporation for not being sufficiently active in addressing some of the illegal Catholic practices which they argued were still going on in too many of York's parish churches. Specifically, the Council accused the Corporation of failing to stop *"the use, service and administration of the sacraments"*. This was to be the first of many such complaints, letters and accusations.

During the opening months of his time as Lord President, Archbishop Young wrote to the Privy Council in Westminster to state that he had serious doubts about the religious conformity and loyalty of the majority of the city's aldermen. The Privy Council were informed that of the current cohort of thirteen men, only two of them, William Watson and Ralph Hall, could confidently be considered to be loyal *"favourers of religion"*. The clear inference here was that the rest were Catholics.

In 1567, the Council of the North ordered one of the more suspect aldermen, James Simpson, to be imprisoned in York Castle. Although the exact charges against Simpson aren't clear, he was one of the men the Archbishop had accused of *"non-favouring"* the Protestant religion in his letter to the Privy Council.

The city's records state that Simpson had not been *"living in the style required of an alderman"*. Although he was released from prison later the same year, James Simpson died shortly afterwards. Following his death, the Privy Council contacted the Corporation regarding the process which should be followed to elect a replacement alderman, suggesting they may have indicated they wanted a more loyalist Protestant man to be chosen in his place.

In the aftermath of Simpson's arrest, and no doubt wishing to be seen in a favourable light by the royal court and in Westminster, Archbishop Young reported to the Privy Council his jurisdiction was now in good order, apart from *"a few gentlemen"* he'd sent to prison.

In 1568, the Archbishop's attention began to turn to the thorny issue of non-attendance of church services. Some Catholics did their best to keep a low profile by attending state Protestant church services as the law directed, before sneaking off to attend an illegal Catholic Mass. Others refused to do so on the basis they considered the Protestant service to be heresy. These more openly dissident and rebellious Catholics were known as recusants.

In an attempt to enforce the new laws, a number of York's citizens were charged with not attending church on Sundays and holy days. Although all were ordered to more appropriately conform to the law in the future, none were severely punished. This would be the first and mildest of many clampdowns on York's Catholic recusant community.

Later in the same year of 1568, Thomas Young died while in Sheffield. His body was returned to York, and he was buried at York Minster. Being a Protestant rather than a Catholic clergyman, Young had been allowed to marry. He did so twice and had at least one son, Sir George Young.

Following his death, the Young family lived at the

Treasurer's House in York. The Archbishop's descendants were responsible for re-designing and changing much of the house to match the form we see today.

Once Archbishop Young was buried, the recently appointed Dean of York, Matthew Hutton, wrote to the government requesting they make haste and quickly appoint a suitable replacement. Dean Hutton was particularly concerned because he had believed Archbishop Young had often acted too leniently towards Catholicism.

Hutton also took a dim view of what he considered to be York's religiously suspect population. In his letter, he described the majority of people in York as being *"ignorant... rude and blind"*. Although Thomas Radcliffe, the Earl of Sussex, was appointed to replace Archbishop Young as the new Lord President of the Council of the North, a swift announcement of a replacement Archbishop of York was not forthcoming.

CHAPTER EIGHTEEN
The Rising of the North

In 1568, Queen Elizabeth's cousin Mary Stuart, the deposed Queen of Scots, escaped after being imprisoned by rebel Scots' lords. She raised a small army and faced down the rebels in battle but was subsequently defeated. After this, Mary travelled to England to request military aid and support from her cousin Elizabeth to help her regain the Scottish throne.

At first, Elizabeth wasn't quite sure what to do about Mary Stuart. Many of Elizabeth's advisors feared, as a Catholic, Mary might gain popular support and become a threat to the English crown. As a result, the former Scots' Queen was held, usually in comfortable conditions and supported by a large entourage, in a series of locations across England.

In July 1568, Mary was transported to Bolton Castle, sixty miles from York in the Yorkshire Dales. As far as we know, Mary didn't visit York, However, in October 1568 a major conference was held in the city to determine her future.

This inquiry or commission was established to examine, amongst other things, whether Mary was guilty of involvement in the murder of her Scottish husband Lord Darnley in 1567. Darnley was the father of her infant son James. She'd been forced to leave the boy behind in Scotland.

Although no records remain of which buildings were used to house the inquiry, it was headed by the Duke of Norfolk and very well attended by both English and Scottish commissioners, including Mary's own representatives. One of the judges was the recently appointed Lord President of the Council of the North, the Earl of Sussex, so it's likely that the hearing was housed in the Council's offices at the King's Manor. Wherever the commission was located, one thing's for sure, the inquiry brought with it a short-lived but significant amount of spending power to York. The inns and alehouses in the city were once again crowded.

Although the deliberations, accusations and defence went on for several weeks, nothing was concluded. A second larger follow-on commission sat in Westminster in November, but this too failed to reach a decisive conclusion. Although nothing had been proven against Mary, it was decided she should remain in custody, and she was moved south from Yorkshire to Tutbury Castle near Derby.

In 1569, a year after the inquiry in York, the city's loyalties were tested to the full as a rebellion began to take shape once again in England's northern counties. This uprising is now known by several names including the Northern Rebellion and the Earls' Rebellion. We'll call it by perhaps its most famous name, the Rising of the North.

The Rising was instigated by two of most important noblemen in the whole of the North of England, Thomas Percy, the Earl of Northumberland, and Charles Neville, the Earl of Westmoreland. The two men harboured both religious and wider grievances.

Following rumours of potential unrest, in October the two Earls were summoned to York by the Earl of Sussex to appear before the Council of the North. Both men denied they were involved in or had heard any reports of an uprising. Although they were allowed to leave the city, the Earl of Sussex continued to harbour suspicions that rebellion was in the air. He wrote to the Privy Council to inform them that he was putting plans in place to take control of York, Hull, Pontefract and

Knaresborough should it become necessary in the event of an uprising.

A few days later, Sussex was markedly more confident that things were now under control, believing the onset of winter would inevitably prevent serious military action at least in the short term. This time he reported to the Privy Council, *"All is very quiet here and the time of year will shortly cool hot rumours".*

However, the Earls of Northumberland and Westmoreland had other ideas. At the beginning of November, they issued a joint proclamation.

"We, Thomas, Earl of Northumberland, and Charles, Earl of Westmorland, the Queen's true and faithful subjects, to all that came of the old Catholic Religion, know ye that we, with many other well-disposed persons, as well of the Nobility as others, have promised our Faith to the Furtherance of this our good meaning. Forasmuch as diverse disordered and well-disposed persons about the Queen's Majesty, have, by their subtle and crafty dealings to advance themselves, overcome in this Realm, the true and Catholic Religion towards God, and by the same abused the Queen, disordered the Realm, and now lastly seek and procure the destruction of the Nobility."

Having outlined their reasoning, the Earls described what they planned to do next.

"We, therefore, have gathered ourselves together to resist by force, and the rather by the help of God and you good people, to see redress of these things amiss, with the restoring of all ancient customs and liberties to God's Church, and this noble Realm; lest if we should not do it ourselves, we might be reformed by strangers, to the great hazard of the state of this our country, whereunto we are all bound. God save the Queen."

Both Northumberland and Westmoreland wished to see a return to Catholicism as the country's state religion. They were also demanding the removal of leading *"crafty"* Protestant advisors to the Queen such as William Cecil, men who they saw as being dangerous enemies to traditional English nobles including themselves.

By ending their statement with *"God save the Queen"*, the Earls had intended to demonstrate their loyalty to the crown. However, they immediately set about raising a large force of armed men, who would be ready to champion and fight for their cause. In addition, the Earls wrote another letter which they sent to the Pope requesting the formal support of the Catholic Church. They hoped this would bring about military support, if needed, from Catholic countries in Europe to help the rebels restore their favoured religion in England.

On 14 November, the Earls marched towards Durham Cathedral. They were supported by a swiftly growing army of men. Taking control of the cathedral, the rebels tore down Protestant imagery and heard Catholic Mass. Advancing south, the rebels soon captured Darlington, Northallerton and Richmond. Wherever they halted, Catholic Mass was heard, and more men were gathered. By the time the rebels had reached Ripon, the size of their army had swelled to approximately six thousand men. Critically, this included sixteen hundred horsemen. Armed cavalry would give them a considerable advantage should they meet resistance.

By this time, reports were reaching York of the sizeable army which appeared to be proceeding towards the city's walls. York's leaders became very aware they would soon be facing the same dilemma as their predecessors during the Pilgrimage of Grace. Should they open the city's gates and let the rebels in, or lock the gates firmly shut and risk an armed assault on the city?

The rebel army continued to move south towards York, before resting at Boroughbridge. On 22 November, they reached Bramham Moor, near Wetherby. At this juncture, it's believed the Earls and their men had two major aims. Their primary goal was to attack Tutbury Castle to free Mary Stuart, the Catholic former Queen of Scots. This would be a major risk. In doing so, the Earls would clearly be displaying their disloyalty not just to Queen Elizabeth's Protestant religion but to the Queen of England herself. A free Mary Stuart with a Catholic army around her would undoubtedly present a serious danger to the English throne.

Although the Earl of Sussex wished to move against the rebels, he was forced to bide his time. There were only around four hundred horsemen under his direct command, so for the time being he remained in York. From there, he wrote another letter to the Privy Council. This time he complained that he was struggling to raise sufficient men to take on the rebels.

Around this time, news reached the Earls that the English authorities had acted to move Mary Stuart forty miles further south from Tutbury to Coventry. Upon discovering the news, the Earls considered Mary was now out of their reach until further forces could be gathered.

As this was the case, they were forced to consider more clearly their second immediate goal. The rebels wanted to capture York, by peaceful means, if possible, but by force if necessary. Once the walled city was under the Earls' control, it would make a perfect fortified base for the rest of their rebellion.

For a time, the people of York waited for an attack to take place. Sussex ordered his horsemen to patrol the banks of the river Ouse. Sentries were sent out to spot the rebel army approaching. The Corporation's leaders could no longer delay their decision. Should they support the Earl of Sussex and the Council of the North or throw their lot behind the Northern Earls and the rebellion?

As we've seen, a good number of Corporation aldermen still harboured Catholic sympathies. It must have been a difficult choice to make. If they didn't let the rebels in, they risked an armed assault of much greater force than the city had faced when it had been attacked by Lord Scrope's Yorkist rebels during the reign of Henry VII. By this time, the Earl of Sussex had temporarily stopped sending messages to the Privy Council, as he was concerned they might be intercepted and read by the rebels.

The Lord Mayor of York in 1569 was the merchant William Beckwith, now serving his second term in mayoral office. The first had been back in 1555 during the Catholic reign of Queen Mary when he'd shown sympathy for the poor by reducing the price of meat in the market.

Lord Mayor Beckwith and his fellow aldermen finally made a momentous decision. The city had opened itself up to the rebels during the Pilgrimage of Grace and subsequently suffered the humiliation of having to kneel down in front of King Henry VIII to beg for the King's forgiveness. They'd also been forced to pay Henry handsomely in gold for their treachery. The current aldermen were determined not to make the same mistake. The Corporation decided the city's gates would not be thrown open to the rebels. Instead, they would remain closed.

Perhaps the decision was made easier because the Earl of Sussex already had a small army in the city. Whatever their reasoning and despite their suspected Catholic allegiances, the Lord Mayor and the aldermen decided to throw their weight behind the Earl of Sussex and the Council of the North. Only four men from York are known to have joined the Earls' army. Instead, York's citizens supported the loyalist forces and began to prepare for an all-out attack on their city. They considered too the potential of having to withstand a long winter siege.

Having discovered York was to be stoutly defended, the Earls and their followers received more bad news. The support they'd expected to receive from the other Catholic nobles wasn't to be. Even worse than that, a royal army was being despatched from the south to engage them.

After spending two days deliberating at Bramham Moor on what their next move should be, the Earls turned their army away from York and moved the men towards Knaresborough. After this, they retreated further back towards their northern heartlands. On the way north, they took the coastal town of Hartlepool, in the hope it could soon become a welcoming port for Spanish reinforcements. Sadly, for the rebels, the Spanish weren't coming either.

Finally, the Earls laid siege to Barnard Castle. Although they captured the town, there was a growing realisation within the group that their rebellion would soon be defeated. With the royal forces closing in on them, the two Earls and a number of their wealthier followers abandoned the main body of their army and fled further north into Scotland. York would be safe.

Once he'd crossed the border, Charles Neville, the Earl of Westmorland, continued travelling onwards until he reached the coast at Aberdeen. From there, he took a boat and sailed across the North Sea, eventually escaping to Flanders. Neville never returned to England. In the aftermath, his lands and assets were seized and forfeited to the crown. The defeated and dejected Earl of Westmorland was forced to live in exile on the continent until his death in 1601.

The Earl of Northumberland, Thomas Percy, wasn't even this fortunate. Having been betrayed, he was captured by a Scottish lord. After being imprisoned, he was sold for a large ransom to Queen Elizabeth's government. We'll cover what happened when he returned to York in 1572 a little later on.

Although the Rising of the North had achieved little, there were grave concerns in the government it might be repeated. Examples had to be made. In his role as Lord President of the Council of the North, the Earl of Sussex issued orders that at least two hundred men who'd followed the Earls were to be executed. One large group of men were hanged together in the marketplace in Ripon.

There was relief for William Beckwith and his fellow aldermen that York hadn't supported the uprising. This must have particularly been the case a short time later when a government commission was held in the city to discuss what should be done about the rebellion. A further eleven rebels were sentenced to death. Four of the men were executed in York.

The 1560s had been something of a turning point in York's Tudor history. For more than ten years, sickness and epidemics had not ravaged the city's population. The establishment of the Ecclesiastical Commission and the permanent housing of the Council of the North in York had brought an influx of wealth and employment. Ouse Bridge may have collapsed, but the city had found the funds and fortitude to rebuild it with a sufficiently strong and robust structure that it would remain standing and span the city's major river for more than two hundred years.

York may not have yet fully embraced the Protestant state religion but, unlike during the Pilgrimage of Grace, the city had demonstrated its loyalty to the crown. The city gates had remained closed to the latest band of rebels, and there was no need for York's leaders to kneel and beg for mercy in front of the Queen. What would the 1570's bring?

CHAPTER NINETEEN
Recusants Part One

Life in York during the latter decades of the sixteenth century was often dominated by one continuing battle. On one side there was the might of the crown, the state, the Church and a section of the city's population who embraced the Protestant religion. On the other were the remaining people who wished to retain the Catholic faith. At times, the second group was supported in their struggle, often surreptitiously, by a number of officials of the Corporation of York.

If Archbishop Thomas Young had still been alive, he could have made a valid claim that it had been his leadership of the Church, the Ecclesiastical Commission and Council of the North which had played a crucial role in ensuring York remained loyal to Queen Elizabeth during the Rising of the North. He'd often however used a relatively subtle approach towards ensuring religious conformity. His actions were certainly less forceful and abrasive than some of his colleagues, particularly the Dean of York Matthew Hutton, would have liked.

In May 1570, some of Dean Hutton's dreams seemed to have come true when Elizabeth announced Edmund Grindal would be the new Archbishop of York. Grindal had previously held the post of chaplain for her avidly Protestant half-brother Edward VI. During Queen Mary's reign, Grindal had been forced to leave the country, fearing for his life. Following his return to England under Elizabeth, he'd served first as the Bishop of London, before being promoted to York.

Like Matthew Hutton, the new Archbishop was both anti-Catholic and Puritan-leaning. As soon as he arrived in York, he became immediately suspicious of large parts of the local population. In a letter to the Queen's senior adviser William Cecil, he complained the local populace was not *"well-affected to Godly religion"* and that far too many of the locals continued to follow *"superstitious practices"*. This meant he thought they were Catholic. In the offices of Minster Yard, this would have been music to the ears of Matthew Hutton.

At the very start of Archbishop Grindal's time in York in July 1570, a dramatic event occurred within the Minster. For a few moments, it appeared the religious reforms Grindal had been planning might come to an end, even before they'd really begun. A man stepped forward towards Grindal and one his colleagues George de Wilton. When a knife appeared in the man's hand, they knew something was wrong. De Wilton was murdered. Alongside him, the new Archbishop Edmund Grindal was wounded.

The perpetrator Thomas Wilson (acting under the alias of Thomas Mountain) was arrested. Although there are limited details of Grindal's would-be killer's motives, it's likely he was a Catholic. Thomas Wilson was tried and sentenced to death.

Wilson though was obviously a resourceful man. While being held inside the Church's Peter prison alongside the Minster, he escaped from his cell. It's recorded that he managed to scale an interior wall, before squeezing into a gap in the eaves. After this, he crawled through a narrow space between the ceilings of the cells and the roof.

Unfortunately for Wilson, somebody heard him moving. As he made his way towards the edge of the building, the alarm was raised. The prison guards appeared, and the prisoner was apprehended. After this, Wilson was searched. He was found to be in possession of a length of rope which he'd made from his own bedding, a hooked nail and a sharp piece of tin plate. He'd used the latter two items to cut the bedding and fashion it into a rope. The escaping prisoner had planned to use the rope to help him descend from the prison's roof. If he'd done this successfully, he may have been able to escape by making off through the streets outside the prison.

After his capture, Wilson was held in one of the dungeon cells. He was chained to a wall and more closely guarded. On the day of his execution, he was taken to the former grounds of St Mary's Abbey where a set of gallows had been constructed. Shortly before his death, the condemned man was allowed to address the crowd which had gathered there. Thomas Wilson shouted, *"God save the Queen"* and then threw himself off the gallows. His dead body was placed and hung in chains at Clifford's Ings.

#

Once he'd recovered from his wounds, Archbishop Grindal didn't dither in his desire to drive changes to the religious customs still being practiced in many of York's churches. If any of the local clergymen refused to be re-educated towards a more Protestant persuasion, he was happy to replace them with more suitable men.

In 1571, the Archbishop issued a set of injunctions which he mandated were to be enforced before his upcoming visitation to the local parish churches. These injunctions included strict instructions to remove a wide range of procedures and items Grindal perceived as being too Catholic in nature. The Archbishop's concern was that far too many of these outdated conventions were still being adhered to in some of York's churches. All were to be eliminated.

Equally, Archbishop Grindal was keen to use the law and the courts within his jurisdiction to address the ongoing and illegal issue of the Catholics who continued to refuse to attend

Church of England services. At this time, Catholics in York and across England and Wales could largely be categorised as falling into one of two main groups.

The first group, sometimes referred to as Church Catholics or Church Papists, attended Church of England services before sneaking off to attend an illegal Catholic Mass in a private residence. In this way, the Church Catholics hoped to avoid the attentions of the authorities and the punishments which might result from their non-conformity.

The other category consisted of much more openly defiant Catholics known as recusants. This group was prepared to take a stand against the law, as they viewed it to be unjust and ungodly. The recusants considered the Church of England's religious service, held in English rather than in Latin, as heresy. In their eyes, the revised church service disregarded too many fundamental elements of Catholic doctrine, such as the failure to recognise all seven of the holy sacraments. As this was the case, they refused to attend, considering whatever punishments they might face on Earth far better than those which they expected to be meted out to Protestants in the afterlife.

During the early months of Archbishop Grindal's tenure in York, there were only a relatively small number of recusancy cases being brought before the courts. We're indebted here and in following sections of the book to the painstaking work of the historian J.C.H. Aveling for his remarkably detailed examination of recusancy related cases in York during the Tudor and Stuart periods. For more information on Aveling's work, please see the bibliography section at the end of the book.

In 1571, Archbishop Grindal established a new Visitation court to address the misdemeanours which had been identified during his promised parish inspections. The Visitation's court books describe the cases which were brought against a number of people in York for regularly not attending their parish church services.

The persons initially charged included:

- George Turton, Oswald Wilkinson and Isabel Wilkinson of St Mary's Castlegate,
- Jane Long of St Nicholas Walmgate,
- John Groves, Emot Halliday and Richard Smuthwaite of Holy Trinity Goodramgate, and
- The husband and wife Thomas Vavasour M.D. and Dorothy Vavasour, also of Holy Trinity, who we'll hear more about shortly.

A number of the above people were requested to attend the Visitation court on multiple occasions. During John Groves' second appearance in the courtroom, for example, he was accompanied by two of his neighbours. In Groves' defence, they testified he'd attended church services and his case was dismissed.

The Visitation court books also include a very interesting case which was brought against the churchwardens at one of the multiple rectories at Bishophill.

The wardens were charged with permitting the *"decay of the church; no decent communication table; their altar stone is not defaced and they suffered a table of image in their church undefined; no pulpit; no sufficient books for Divine service"*.

In response to the Visitation court's findings, the accused promised they'd act quickly to get their church back into good shape. In the wardens' defence, the court heard how, *"They say they have now provided a table and decent cup of silver and pulpit and will get the books to put all right and certify it."*

Perhaps though it was John Pulleyn, the vicar at Bishophill, who was the real problem rather than his churchwardens. The Visitation court book indicates Pulleyn came before the court, accused of keeping *"an alehouse in the vicarage"*. In part of his admonishment, Pulleyn was instructed, *"to avoid the suspicious company of women"*. We don't know if he did, or if he didn't do this, but it sounds like he was an interesting vicar.

Some of the people accused by the Visitation court were cited afterwards to attend the official Ecclesiastical High Commission court. In June 1571, the Commission heard the case of an important York gentleman called Edward Besley. During Queen Mary's reign, Besley had been the Member of Parliament for each of Ripon, Thirsk and Scarborough. In 1556, he'd also been appointed into two important roles in York, the clerk for York Castle and, in succession to his father, the city's official solicitor.

Although he was clearly a wealthy man and had influence, Besley, his second wife Bridget (née Nelson) and other members of their family were all Catholic. For example, one of Besley's relatives (probably his son), George Besley, would go on to become a Catholic seminary priest and be executed for treason in 1591.

In the coming years, Besley was a frequent visitor to York's courts and prisons, if not to the city's churches. Along with another fellow accused man, Stephen Branton, the High Commission stated Besley *"refuses expressly to communicate or come to the church"*. After being *"committed to the custody of the sheriffs of York"*, both men were sent to prison.

Archbishop Grindal remained convinced that the number of recusants in York was still far higher than the actual volume of cases being brought before the courts. When he demanded the Corporation take further action, the aldermen reluctantly promised to work more closely with York's parishes to create a more accurate and complete list of church absentees. However, if the lists were properly compiled, there was a risk they might contain the names of a number of the aldermen as well as their wider families.

Under further pressure from the Archbishop, Dean Hutton and the Council of the North, the Corporation reluctantly abolished the annual Corpus Christi plays and the city's Yuletide festivities. Both had been criticised as being overly superstitious Catholic traditions by the Council of the North and the Ecclesiastical High Commission.

In 1572, the Earl of Sussex left York to take up a position as the Lord Chamberlain in London. The important role of Lord President of the Council of the North was passed onto Henry Hastings, the third Earl of Huntingdon. Hastings's wife Katherine was the daughter of the Duke of Northumberland, the man who'd been executed for attempting to place Lady Jane Grey on the English throne.

Like Archbishop Grindal and Dean Hutton, Huntingdon was a fervent Protestant. The trio now began to work closely together to crack down on what they saw as the continued unacceptable Catholic practices and activities which were somehow still going on in York despite all the good work of the Visitation and Ecclesiastical courts.

In the same year, the Scots lord who had imprisoned Thomas Percy, the Earl of Northumberland, after the unsuccessful Rising of the North, agreed financial terms with Queen Elizabeth and her advisors for the Earl's *"release"* from custody. Following a huge payment of £2,000, Northumberland was handed over to the English authorities. He was transported south from Scotland and held in prison in York.

Thomas Percy had already been sentenced to death for his role in the Rising of the North. A large scaffold was erected on the Pavement in the centre of the city. In a clear warning of would happen next to any others who dared to rise up and rebel against the Queen, the Earl was publicly beheaded. To maximise the crowds present, the execution took place on a market day.

As tradition dictated for traitors, Percy's severed head was later stuck onto a spike. It was then placed on the top of a pole which was held up high over Micklegate Bar for all visitors to York to see as they entered the city. The location was known locally as traitor's gate.

According to the *Antiquities of York*, the remainder of the Earl's *"body was buried in Christ's Church by two of his servants and three women"*. Two years later, Thomas Percy's head was mysteriously removed from the top of Micklegate Bar by *"persons unknown"*.

Back in 1572, a curious case was brought before the Ecclesiastical High Commission. A local saddler called William Tessimond was placed into custody by the Sheriffs of York. He'd been found to be in possession of a chest. Inside the trunk was a folded piece of paper. This contained a set of trimmed whiskers. Written on the paper were the words: *"This is the hair of the good Earl of Northumberland Lord Percy"*.

When questioned, Tessimond admitted he'd shaved the hair off the beard of the decapitated head of the Earl after he'd been executed. To achieve this, he'd have had to bribe the guards to gain access to the toll booth on Ouse Bridge where the Earl's head was being stored before being placed on display above Micklegate Bar.

The case indicates the fondness some Catholics still had for owning relics which were made from body parts of dead martyrs. This was one of the *"superstitious"* practices Thomas Cromwell had previously attempted to ban during the reign of Henry VIII. Decades later under Elizabeth I, Archbishop Grindal and the Protestant authorities in York were equally keen to stamp it out.

In the court, Tessimond also confessed to having not attended church, *"He did not communicate nor come to the church... this two or three years, and that the cause thereof was his misliking for the order of the service for that it is not like the order of service of the Catholic Church"*. Having been found guilty of possessing relics and the crime of recusancy, Tessimond was sent to prison.

Rather more charitably, William Tessimond was released from gaol on licence on the next Christmas Day until the beginning of February. However, his release was accompanied by a condition. Tessimond was instructed that he must go to church and take communion during the time he was free.

Whether he did or didn't attend the subsequent church services during this time isn't recorded, but it seems unlikely. The following June, Tessimond was once again allowed to leave prison. After this, he was *"asked to go to church"*. When he steadfastly refused, he lost his liberty once more and was swiftly *"sent back to prison"*. It's easy to forget sometimes these days just how important religion was to so many people during this period.

CHAPTER TWENTY
Earthquake!

The religious antipathy felt between Protestants and Catholics wasn't the only thing experienced by people in York in the 1570's. At five o'clock in the early evening of February 26 in 1575, the city was struck by a relatively major earthquake.

The renowned Tudor historian John Stow wrote afterwards of the wide-ranging effects of the quake. He compiled his notes meticulously from a series of local reports which had been recorded in various parts of the country. Some of these reports had originated in locations two or three hundred miles away from each other. It appears significant tremors were felt across much of England and Wales in a diagonal direction. The north-eastern extent of the quake was in Durham, while tremors were felt across much of the North of England, down through the Midlands, into Northeast Wales and as far south-west in England as Bristol.

In his account, Stow reports how people in places as far distant as York, Hereford and Bristol fled from their homes in fear that the buildings would fall down and collapse upon them. In Wales, a section of Ruthin castle collapsed. A bell began ringing out in Denbigh of its own accord. In Shrewsbury, there were detailed reports that the disturbance consisted of a main quake followed by a series of aftershocks which lasted for over half an hour.

The most serious account of damage in Yorkshire originated in Hatfield near Doncaster, thirty miles south of York.

Here, it was reported that there was a wide scale panic and mass hysteria in the streets, as a number of barns collapsed. A gable end of the town's Manor Hall was badly damaged.

Although there was initially a level of panic in York, the main impact on the city appears to have been on people's mental state rather than any physical damage or injury. Shortly after the quake, Archbishop Grindal wrote to the Archbishop of Canterbury Matthew Parker.

In his letter, Grindal described how a major earthquake had been felt across much of the Midlands and the North, including in Yorkshire, Lancashire, Durham and Nottinghamshire. After describing the quake, Grindal reassured Archbishop Parker that no serious physical damage had been done around the Minster, as *"it shook not down so much as a tile"*.

However, the Archbishop of York did have a concern. The reason he raised the earthquake in the letter was the effect it seemed to be having on the mental state of some of York's people, many of whom he still regarded with suspicion, if not downright hostility, for being *"superstitious"* Catholics.

Archbishop Grindal explained to Parker how the earthquake had affected parts of the city's population, placing them *"in great fear of some greater matter to follow… fearing, as it seems, this present earthquake to portend the Queen's death"*.

The reason for such a collective premonition was due to the fact that news had reached York that a similar earthquake had been felt around London shortly prior to the death of Elizabeth's predecessor and half-brother Edward VI. Archbishop Parker was having none of it, particularly as no tremors had even been felt in the south-eastern parts of the country.

In his reply to Archbishop Grindal, he wrote, *"As for the earthquake, I heard not of it, nor was it felt of here. Deus est faciat quod bonum est in oculis suis."*

The final line of the Archbishop of Canterbury's letter was

in Latin. His words translate into English as *"God does what is good in his eyes."* Whatever he may have meant by this, the fears of York's people were eventually assuaged. Their houses hadn't collapsed upon them, and the Queen of England didn't die in the aftermath.

CHAPTER TWENTY-ONE
Guy Fawkes's Schooldays

The decade of the 1570's also saw the birth and childhood of one of York's most famous, or perhaps infamous, Tudor residents. Guy Fawkes was born in York in April in the year of 1570, probably a few yards away from York Minster. Having said that, there has been a level of debate down the years about the exact location of his birthplace.

It's most likely that Guy was born in either High Petergate (at the site of today's Guy Fawkes Inn) or just around the corner in Stonegate (where a plaque on the wall states his parents once lived). I was told in one of my history talks that these claims were both in error and that Guy had actually been born a few miles downstream along the river Ouse in Bishopthorpe.

Guy's family are known to have owned property in Bishopthorpe, but it's much more likely he was born in the centre of York. Traditionally in Tudor times children were baptised in their local parish church on the third day after their birth. The records show that Guy was baptised in St Michel le Belfry next to York Minster on 16 April, so it's very probable he was born in the city centre, and that the date of his birth was 13 April 1570.

As previously described, Guy's great grandfather William Harrington was the Lord Mayor of York at the time of the Pilgrimage of Grace. He was the man who had permitted the rebels to enter the city. In doing so, he probably saved York from an armed assault, but not from the wrath of Queen Elizabeth's father Henry VIII. William Harrington's daughter Ellen married an ecclesiastical lawyer named William Fawkes. It's believed William Fawkes was related to the Fawkes family of Farnley near Otley. If you're interested in this branch of the Fawkes family and their history, group visits can be arranged to their family home in Farnley Hall where you'll be able to find out much more.

William and Ellen had a son called Edward Fawkes. When Edward grew up, he became an advocate in the Protestant Consistory Court of the Archbishop of York. The family of Edward's wife Edith (née Jackson or possibly Blake) may have had Catholic leanings and ties to the village of Scotton near Knaresborough.

Edward and Edith Fawkes had four children. Sadly, their first-born Anne died shortly after her birth in 1568. The couple's only son Guy was born in 1570. He was followed by two sisters, a second Anne in 1572 and Elizabeth in 1575. With Edward Fawkes's role in the Archbishop's court, as a young boy Guy was raised in a Protestant household. Along with his family and neighbours, Guy Fawkes attended the Protestant Church of England services at their nearby St Michel le Belfry parish church.

As there are no surviving school records from this time, we don't know exactly at which age Guy started school. We do know that he became a pupil at St Peter's school, which had recently been reopened by the Church in the city. The school accepted local boys such as Guy, who attended on a day basis, and boarders from further afield. At this time, the school wasn't located in Bootham where it is today but at the Horse Fair, a ten-minute walk from Guy's family's home near to York Minster.

When St Peter's was re-established by the Church during the reign of Queen Mary, the intention was to create a strictly Catholic seat of learning. Under Queen Elizabeth, the focus had changed to ensure teaching and learning was based upon delivering a reformist Protestant education. One of the Archbishops of York described the school as *"The only good school in this great city"*. Perhaps he fancied himself as an early Ofsted inspector of schools?

However, St Peter's wasn't without its problems. One of the headmasters, John Fletcher, had previously been the head teacher at York's rival grammar school which had been established by the flip-flopping Catholic-Protestant-Catholic Archbishop Holgate. Unfortunately for the Church, Fletcher seems to have brought with him to St Peter's (at least to their mind) some rather suspect religious tendencies.

Not long after he'd become the headmaster at St Peter's, John Fletcher was sacked due to suspicions that he was a practicing Catholic. After his dismissal, he was despatched to prison. Fletcher spent almost two decades languishing in various gaols for his non-conformist religious beliefs. At first, he was interred inside York Minster's Peter Prison but, having been found guilty of *"abusing"* the prison and causing *"by his doings the offence of many"*, he was *"removed to Ripon to be kept close prisoner"*.

John Fletcher's successor was announced in 1575. It was perhaps quite a remarkable choice. Some historians believe that the new head teacher John Pulleyn was the same man who'd been cited four years earlier by the visitation courts for running an *"alehouse in the vicarage"*. If this was the case, it makes you wonder about the diligence of the selection committee. Maybe John Pulleyn didn't mention the fact he'd been charged whilst at the rectory at Bishophill or instructed by the courts *"to avoid the suspicious company of women"*. The population of York was so much smaller at the time. Surely the people recruiting him would have known about his background.

Perhaps he was a changed man, or perhaps the selection

committee focused mostly on the instructions which had been given to them in 1571 by Archbishop Grindal. His orders had been that all schoolmasters should be of good and sincere religion, not use vain books, nor teach anything contrary to the state faith. Either way, John Pulleyn remained in his position at St Peter's for another fifteen years.

As such, he would have been the headmaster of the school for the whole time Guy was a pupil there. With only two masters teaching at the school, John Pulleyn would have had had a significant influence on young Guy Fawkes's life.

Before we take a deeper look into Guy's schooldays, it is worth examining what school was like for the boys (there were only boys) in Tudor York's grammar schools. The school day started early, usually around six thirty or seven in the morning, and finished late in the early evening around six o'clock over the summer and five o'clock in the darker evenings of the winter. If they couldn't do so already, the boys were taught to read and write. They studied religion and classics subjects, including Latin, Hebrew and Greek. The boys attended religious services and those with the best singing voices were selected to sing in choirs at local churches and major events.

Discipline inside and outside the school was strict. The boys could and would be punished for anything which the schoolmasters or the Church deemed to be poor behaviour. In 1566, a group of pupils from St Peter's were caught playing *"football within the cathedral church of York"*. It appears kicking a ball around the grounds of the Minster wasn't the done thing. Two of the boys, Oswald Atkinson and Christopher Dobson, were each given six strokes of the birch. Young Atkinson was punished further by being placed in the stocks. Four centuries later, I accidentally smashed a canteen window with a football at my primary school. Thankfully, I had a different headmaster. My only punishment was a telling off.

Whether it came solely from the boys or also from his teachers, Guy Fawkes now found himself being increasingly exposed to Catholic influences at St Peter's. His fellow pupils at this time included two brothers from the East Riding of Yorkshire. John (or Jack) Wright was two years older than Guy, while his younger brother Christopher (or Kit) was the same age. The Wrights hailed from a well-known family of Catholic recusants, all of whom refused to attend services in the Protestant Church.

In 1605, Jack and Kit would go on to play an instrumental role in recruiting Guy Fawkes to the Gunpowder Plot. Both men, like Guy, would lay down their lives for their Catholic cause after the group failed to assassinate Queen Elizabeth's successor, James I. In addition, by that time their sister Martha Wright had married another Gunpowder Plotter, Thomas Percy, a distant cousin of the Earl of Northumberland. Percy was also killed by the Protestant authorities.

The Catholic contingent at St Peter's didn't stop there. Another one of Guy's fellow pupils was Oswald Tessimond. You may recall Oswald's father William. He was the fellow who'd been arrested and imprisoned for refusing to go to church and snipping off the Earl of Northumberland's beard.

When William's son Oswald left St Peter's, he made his way to the continent to train to become a Catholic priest. After re-entering England, Oswald became part of a growing illegal network of missionary Catholic priests. Following the Gunpowder Plot, Father Tessimond was accused of supporting the conspiracy and a warrant was issued for his arrest. Thankfully for him, he managed to escape to the relative safety of the continent where he went on to write an important account of what had happened. This is perhaps of particular interest because it was written by one of the losers rather than the winners.

The family of another of Guy's classmates, Edward Oldcorne, also featured regularly in York's recusancy cases in court. Just like Tessimond, Oldcorne later left England to join the Catholic priesthood and returned to England undercover. He too was suspected of being connected to the Gunpowder Plot but, unlike Father Tessimond, Father Oldcorne wasn't quite as lucky. Despite the apparent dearth of evidence against him, he was arrested, tried for his links to the Plot and executed for treason in 1606.

Back in 1578 when Guy was only eight years old, his father Edward died. In the coming years, Guy's mother Edith married again. Her second husband was a Catholic man from Scotton called Dionysius Bainbridge. With Catholic influences all around him both at home and at school, it's little wonder then at some stage during his youth Guy converted to the Catholic faith. We'll shortly examine what else the young Guy Fawkes may have witnessed in York which could have radicalised him sufficiently to want to blow up Parliament and kill the King of England.

Two decades before the Gunpowder Plot, Guy left St Peter's school. He also left York. After leaving Yorkshire behind, he spent several years near to the south coast of England in Sussex working in the household of the Viscount Montagues, one of the country's leading Catholic families. Their home, the original Cowdray House, was a fine building at the time, although it's a picturesque ruin these days. For some unknown reason, the first Viscount Montague sacked Guy from his role. However, when he died shortly afterwards, the second Viscount Montague swiftly re-employed him.

In 1590 Guy returned home, albeit briefly, to Yorkshire. Some historians believe that during the time he was there, Guy married a Maria Pulleyn from Scotton and the couple had a baby son named Thomas. This may or may not be true. At the time of writing no categorical documented evidence of this has been uncovered. If the marriage did happen, it's likely Martha and Thomas both died, possibly during childbirth.

When Guy turned twenty-one years old in April 1571, he came of age and took possession of what was left of his father's estate. He sold off several of the family's properties in and around York and left England to travel to mainland Europe. Unlike Oswald Tessimond or Edward Oldcorne, Guy had no wish to enter a holy order or train to become a Catholic priest. Instead, he took the second main avenue open to young a Catholic Englishman at the time who'd become disenchanted with their country and the Protestant state religion.

Guy took a boat probably from Hull to the Low Countries. Once there, he enlisted in one of the English units of the Spanish army. At this time, much of modern-day Belgium and the Netherlands were part of the wider Spanish Empire. A bloody civil war was taking place between Protestant rebels in the local Dutch and Flemish populations and their Spanish masters and Catholic supporters.

Deciding to join the fight on the side of the Catholic Spanish, perhaps Guy considered this to be a holy war. Whatever his motivations were, fighting for the Spanish army would clearly be viewed as treason in his homeland. This was barely three years since the Spanish Armada had unsuccessfully attempted to lead a Catholic invasion of England. Little is known of Guy's service record, other than he became an explosives expert, a critical skill when so many of the battles included siege warfare against walled towns. It was also a skill which might prove to be valuable in future.

Guy continued to fight for the Spanish army until around 1603. After this time, he became a secret envoy, effectively a spy, carrying messages between leading English Catholic dissidents in the Low Countries and the Spanish authorities in Madrid. During this period, he was recommended to the leader of the Gunpowder Plot, Robert Catesby, by his old friends from York, the Wright brothers.

Having recently changed his first name from Guy to Guido, Fawkes was approached in Madrid by Catesby's right hand man Thomas Wintour. When he was asked to join them, Guido opted to throw in his lot with the small band of conspirators led by Robert Catesby in what we now know as the Gunpowder Plot. The rest as they say is history.

If you'd like to read an engaging book about the history of the Gunpowder Plot, I'd strongly recommend Lady Antonia Fraser's excellent work. For a well-researched and very readable biography of Guy Fawkes, Nick Holland's book is a very good choice.

Lastly, if you might also wish to read an exciting and highly rated novel about Guy Fawkes's youth set in the dark streets of Tudor York, I've been reliably informed *"The Pearl of York, Treason and Plot"* is also excellent. It merges the fictional tale of a youthful Guy with the tragic true-life story of Margaret Clitherow, which we'll cover shortly.

Author self-promotion alert! *"The Pearl of York, Treason and Plot"* is admittedly one of my own novels but from all the positive reviews, lots of people seem to like it. If you do read it, please let me know what you think about it. Just like this book, the profits are donated to St Leonard's Hospice in York, the modern-day equivalent of St Leonard's Hospital, which was closed during the Dissolution by Thomas Cromwell and Henry VIII. These days, the hospice staff do such fantastic work. I'm very happy to support them.

CHAPTER TWENTY-TWO
Recusants Part Two

Guy Fawkes and his mother Edith weren't the only people in York during the middle and later years of Queen Elizabeth I's reign to find themselves favouring Catholicism over the state religion. Earlier, we mentioned that Dr Thomas and his wife Dorothy Vavasour had been brought before the Visitation court for missing church services.

Thomas Vavasour was related to one of the leading families in Tudor Yorkshire, the Vavasours of Hazlewood Castle. If you visit Hazlewood Castle these days, it's now a hotel. Be sure to check out the framed family tree on display at the back of the reception area. If you look very carefully, you should be able to make out the names of Dorothy and Thomas Vavasour MD somewhere in the middle.

In the thirteenth century, Tadcaster stone from one of the Vavasours' quarries was used to construct York Minster. For several centuries afterwards, male members of the Vavasour family were regularly elevated to the eminent position of the High Sheriff of Yorkshire.

Sir William Vavasour, for example, held the role in 1548 and 1563. His son John hosted Mary Queen of Scots when she stayed overnight at Hazlewood Castle in 1569. This was during her journey from Bolton Castle to Tutbury. A few miles away in nearby York, the official commission was being held to determine her fate.

This was the nearest Mary Stuart would ever get to York.

At least while she was in Hazlewood Castle, Mary was being cared for by sympathetic hosts. The Vavasours retained and cherished their Catholicism. In the decades to come, the Vavasours of Hazlewood Castle would become very well known, and sometimes persecuted and prosecuted, for Catholic recusancy.

As a young man, Thomas Vavasour had studied at Cambridge University. While he was in Cambridge, he encountered the future Archbishop of York Edmund Grindal. The two men didn't see eye to eye on many issues. This didn't bode well for Thomas Vavasour when he would later live in York. Edmund Grindal is quoted as having discounted his fellow student for being *"disdainful, and eluding arguments with irrision, when he was not able to solute the same by learning"*.

After Cambridge, Thomas Vavasour left the country for some time and studied medicine (and perhaps religion) in Venice in Italy, before returning to England during the reign of Queen Mary. In 1556, he was given a license by the Royal College of Physicians to practice as a medical doctor.

After marrying Dorothy (née Kent), he took up residence in York. The couple lived in a house in the parish of Holy Trinity, Goodramgate. While they were there, amongst other things, they began to support local women through the rigours of childbirth. One of those who is believed to have availed herself of the Vavasours' maternity services was Margaret Clitherow. It's believed Dorothy Vavasour supported Margaret when she gave birth to her eldest two children, her son Henry and daughter Anne.

In the early years of Elizabeth's reign in the 1560's, Thomas and Dorothy Vavasour had done little to hide their strong devotion to the Catholic faith. During this decade, this had been less of a problem. Often, the Corporation of York and York's churchwardens turned a blind eye to those who avoided church services. People's names weren't always placed upon the official recusancy lists, and sometimes they were taken off.

By the time of the 1570's things were changing. Under increasing pressure and a growing number of official missives from the Council of the North, Dean Hutton and Archbishop Grindal, the situation was different. After being cited by the Visitation court in 1571 for their non-attendance of parish church services, the Vavasours were referred, along with a number of other of York's citizens, to attend the more senior court of the Ecclesiastical High Commission.

However, there was some confusion during this process. At first, the couple weren't formally summonsed to appear in the court. Instead, the two Sheriffs of York were *"fined because they did not serve the court's attachments on these persons"*. The reasons the Sheriffs didn't act in the way the court had wished is unknown. It could have been down to Catholic sympathies, an instruction from one or more of York's aldermen or something else altogether.

The Sheriffs of York at the time were Thomas Middleton and Henry Maye. These are interesting names. For example, Thomas Middleton was the name of Margaret Clitherow's birth father. As mentioned above, Margaret had been supported by the Vavasours when she'd given birth to her children.

However, this Thomas Middleton who was one of the Sheriffs in 1570/71 wasn't her father. We know this as Margaret's birth father, had already served his own term as a Sheriff in 1564/65. More conclusively, he'd died a few years earlier in 1567. The second Thomas Middleton wasn't Margaret's brother, but he may have been a relative.

Margaret Clitherow's connection to the second Sheriff Henry Maye was even closer. Shortly after Margaret's father Thomas Middleton died, her mother Jane remarried. Jane's new husband was a much younger man, an immigrant from the south coast of England called... Henry Maye.

After his marriage, Henry became Margaret Clitherow's (then Margaret Middleton's) stepfather. Despite being half his wife's age and coming from a lower social class, Henry Maye quickly made good use of his new family's connections and wealth. He closed down the Middletons' wax chandlery in Davygate (near to where the famous Betty's cafe is today), gained a licence to trade alcohol, converted the family home into a tavern, joined the Common Council and became a Sheriff.

From what we know of Henry Maye's later years, he was certainly no Catholic sympathiser. It's quite possible the real reason the Vavasours and some of the others weren't summonsed to appear in the Ecclesiastical court wasn't due to any attempt to aid them, but simply down to incompetence or a flaw in the process. Either way Henry Maye and the other Thomas Middleton were fined for their troubles.

Archbishop Grindal, Dean Hutton and Lord President Huntingdon continued to pile pressure on the Corporation of York to take a stronger and firmer stand against the city's Catholics. They particularly wanted greater action to be taken against York's openly recusant citizens such as the Vavasours. From 1573 onwards, all new Lord Mayors and Sheriffs of York were forced to swear an Oath of Supremacy to the Queen in addition to their own oath of office. The Council of the North was sending a signal to the Corporation. If its senior officers stepped out of line, then consequences would follow.

In November 1574, Thomas Vavasour was finally brought before the Ecclesiastical High Commission. He was accused of refusing to go to church and also of harbouring *"openly papistical, unsound and idolatrous opinions"*. What's more, the court heard he was *"much inclined to seduce others"* not to attend church services. This was a very serious accusation.

When Dr Vavasour was found guilty, he was sentenced to

serve a spell in a York prison cell under the custody of one of the then current Sheriffs Robert Brooke. Shortly afterwards, however, he was transferred to serve the rest of his sentence in Hull. This was about the same time as the ex-schoolmaster John Fletcher was transferred from York to Ripon. Perhaps this pair of learned men had been such a bad influence on their fellow inmates that they'd both been sent away from the city in a concerted action.

Conditions were far from ideal in most prisons during the Tudor period, but Hull gaol had a reputation for being one of the worst. By August 1575, Thomas Vavasour had already become ill. The records describe him as being *"sickly and diseased"*. When the doctor's condition was brought to the attention of the Ecclesiastical High Commission, the court decided to permit his conditional and temporary release, with the promise of his return to prison covered by a bond. The commissioners also made an order for Thomas to be placed into the custody of his brother William Vavasour.

Thomas was confined to William's house until October to give him time to recover from his illness. The period of this release was extended several times, each one covered by a substantially increased bond, with it finally reaching as high as a huge £200. Later, Thomas was allowed to return to his own home in York for a period, under the condition he was only allowed *"to see his own household"*. The authorities were clearly concerned of the risks of him persuading other people, such as his neighbours, to not attend church.

Finally in May 1577, Thomas was sent back to prison in Hull. There he was placed in a shared cell with a group of Catholic priests who'd been recently imprisoned. Like many of the other inmates in Hull gaol, some of these priests had already gone down with ailments. Dr Vavasour was permitted to put his medical skills to good use and allowed to treat his fellow prisoners, but only *"if it be done in the keeper's hearing"*.

While Dr Vavasour was languishing in his prison cell or sick bed, his wife Dorothy was keeping herself busy. She'd continued to use the family's home in York to provide midwifery services to local women. It's believed she also used this critical and concerning time in many of the women's lives to persuade some of their number to convert or revert to Catholicism.

Records from this time show York had a growing and relatively large number of female recusants, with many young women such as Margaret Clitherow joining their ranks. There's every possibility the Vavasours' maternity clinic played an important role in this, acting as a fertile breeding ground for female recusancy.

CHAPTER TWENTY-THREE
The Angry Archbishop

After all his good work as a scourge of Catholicism and Catholics in York, in 1575 Edmund Grindal was promoted to the lofty heights of Archbishop of Canterbury. A short gap followed. During this time York was temporarily left without an archbishop. The official residence of the Archbishop of York was, and still is, Bishopthorpe Palace. As the palace was now temporarily empty, the Earl of Huntingdon saw an opportunity. Perhaps he'd become tired of city centre life. He moved himself and his wife Katherine out of the Council of the North's lodgings at the King's Manor and into the grander environs of the archbishop's palace.

Two years later in 1577, the Earl of Huntingdon received a letter from the Queen's adviser William Cecil. This letter informed the Earl that the Queen had finally made a decision about who to appoint as York's new archbishop. Grindal's successor was going to be the Bishop of London Edwin Sandys. Huntingdon found himself in a rather awkward position. It appeared he liked his new home very much. The dilemma was exacerbated when a section of William Cecil's letter specifically requested the Earl's help and support for moving Archbishop Sandys's office and family into the Church's palaces at Bishopthorpe and Cawood.

Just like one of his predecessors, Robert Holgate, Edwin Sandys had taken the opportunity to get married during the reign of Edward VI. When Edward died and his half-sister Mary was crowned Queen of England, Holgate found himself in prison. He quickly renounced his marriage and his Protestantism. Edwin Sandys, however, would do no such thing.

At the beginning of Mary's reign, Sandys found himself immediately in trouble. It wasn't just the fact he was a Protestant, and he had a wife. Inadvertently, Sandys had become embroiled in the plot to replace King Edward with Lady Jane Grey.

In Cambridge, he'd preached a sermon to some of Lady Jane's supporters. Later, he argued he'd only done so under duress. Nevertheless, after Mary's coronation, Sandys was arrested. He was locked up in a cell in the Tower of London, before being transferred to the Marshalsea gaol.

With the very real threat of execution looming over him, Sandys managed to escape from the Marshalsea. Aided by his friends, he evaded his Catholic captors, smuggled himself to the coast and found a boat. After this, he crossed the English Channel.

In the coming months, Sandys sent word to his wife Mary and their infant son James. Shortly after they answered his call and joined him in his exile in Strasbourg, both fell ill with bubonic plague and died. If Edwin Sandys harboured anti-Catholic feelings, perhaps he had more reason to do so than many of his fellow Protestant clergymen.

After Elizabeth acceded to the throne in 1558, Sandys was welcomed back into England where he was made a bishop. His first appointment was in Worcester, before he was promoted to the position of the Bishop of London. Following his return to England, Sandys had remarried. By the time of his journey north to York, he was accompanied by his second wife Cicely and their eight children. A ninth would soon follow in York one year later.

In addition to a large family, Archbishop Sandys arrived in York with a negative view of the city's people, as well as many of those who lived in the northern counties in general. Reflecting upon his new diocese, he wrote *"where there is backwardness in knowledge, there must also be a weakness of faith"*.

Following his arrival in York, Sandys wrote a letter to the Privy council. In this, he reported the local inhabitants were *"stiff-necked, wilful and obstinate"*. It appears that most of the new Archbishops of York around this time held quite dim views of Yorkshire people.

Edwin Sandys also brought with him a reputation for being belligerent. During his time in York, he fell out with just about everyone he met there. One of his first major arguments was with one of the men who we may have expected to have been his greatest ally. His initial difference of opinion with the Earl of Huntingdon was not down to any discrepancy in state or religious policy. Instead, it was based around a purely domestic matter. The newly arrived Archbishop of York wanted the well-established Lord President of the Council of the North out of his palace, and he wanted him out quickly.

Archbishop Sandys wrote a long letter to Huntingdon listing ten reasons why the Earl and his wife should swiftly vacate the premises, in order for Sandys and his own family to move in in their stead. In the letter, Sandys outlined that the palace was owned by the Church and not by the crown, hence the Earl had no right to be there. He also pointed out that the location enabled himself as Archbishop to provide hospitality to the Church's guests in a position which was conveniently close to York.

The Earl of Huntingdon was furious. He argued that the Sandys family could and should reside very comfortably in the Church's other palace down the river Ouse at Cawood, the building which had been refurbished by Thomas Wolsey during his downfall. Sandys' counter was that he had no wish to be located eight or so miles further away from York. He also said that the close proximity of Bishopthorpe to York limited the distance and discomfort a man of his *"great years"* would have to travel, when compared to Cawood. When he arrived in York, Sandys was around sixty. Huntingdon was fifteen years his junior.

With his arguments appearing to be failing, the Earl of Huntingdon wrote a long letter of complaint to the Queen's principal secretary Francis Walsingham. In this letter, he highlighted how dissatisfied he was with the situation. One of Huntingdon's particular concerns was that the Archbishop's staff had given him only fifteen days' notice to get out of Bishopthorpe, which he considered to be unreasonable and unacceptable.

The Earl's words and letters made little difference. Before long, he was forced to transfer his home, office and wife back to the King's Manor. Soon afterwards, Sandys moved with his family into Bishopthorpe. The frosty start to the two men's relationship would soon become the norm.

Two years after they'd initially fallen out, Archbishop Sandys wrote to William Cecil, warning him not to attempt any reconciliation between the Earl and himself. In the Archbishop's opinion, any conciliatory words which might be offered by Huntingdon would be purely from *"the lips and not from the heart"*. Some other things must have gone on between the pair in the meantime, as the Archbishop wrote that he deplored the Earl's actions and the *"manifold wrongs done unto me"*.

If there was a third man in this relationship, it was the Dean of York, Matthew Hutton. Although it may have been logical to assume the two churchmen would have formed a closer alliance, this wasn't the case. Dean Hutton had been a staunch ally of Archbishop Grindal's. Both men had created and maintained a strong relationship with the Earl of Huntingdon. However, this was not to be the same with Edwin Sandys.

When Sandys had been appointed as the Bishop of London,

Matthew Hutton had been one of his rival candidates vying for the role. By the time Sandys was appointed Archbishop of York, a level of distrust and enmity had already developed between the two men.

Dissatisfied with the situation, Archbishop Sandys attempted to get Dean Hutton moved away from his York diocese. When a vacancy came up for a new Dean in Lichfield in the Midlands, Sandys wrote a recommendation that Hutton should be transferred south and appointed to the role, but the move wasn't permitted.

Matthew Hutton was left unimpressed and reacted badly. In another letter to Willian Cecil, the Archbishop reported that Dean Hutton was motivated by *"malice towards me and mine"* and that *"the Dean spits his venom still"*. One of Sandys' gripes was that Hutton had blocked him from arranging the same sort of visitation to York's parish churches that Archbishop Grindal had previously carried out.

At times, both men accused each other of non-worthy religious behaviour. Hutton hinted that Sandys had Papist tendencies, while Sandys accused the Dean of having Puritanical leanings. Of the two accusations, the latter seems much more likely to have been closer to the truth. Sandys also claimed Hutton was responsible for financial irregularities, alleging that the Dean had purchased large swathes of land for his own personal use and benefit, rather than for the Church.

The two men constantly took opposing sides in a number of wider arguments. The level of ill feeling between the pair continued unabated during the whole period of Archbishop Sandys' tenure in York.

CHAPTER TWENTY-FOUR
Recusants Part Three

Although Archbishop Sandys had fallen out with both the Earl of Huntingdon and Dean Hutton, if there was one topic they fundamentally all agreed upon it was their opposition to Catholic practices, including recusancy. All three of the men were keen to push for an even stronger crackdown on York's surviving Catholic community. In the late 1570's and early 1580's, the ongoing argument between the Council of the North and the Corporation of York regarding the punishment of York's Catholics reached its peak.

The volume of recusancy cases being heard in York's courts was rising. One interesting aspect of this was that it was often the woman of the household rather than the man who was being brought to court. Sometimes this was because the whole family were Catholic, but they had made a collective decision that they couldn't afford to risk losing their livelihood, which might happen if the husband was arrested and sent to jail. This being the case, the wife and mother often took a stand on their family's behalf by refusing to go to church in lieu of them all. Of course, this wasn't always the case. Religious differences sometimes split certain families down the middle.

In December 1575, Foxgaile Geldard, Frances Hall and Isabel Porter were all charged in York for non-attendance of church services. Although the court commissioners outlined that they were minded to pardon the women, they had one condition. The trio had to first promise they'd cease their recusancy and return to the Church on a regular basis. When the women all refused, each was sentenced to prison. Foxgaile Geldard was sent to York Castle, while Hall and Porter were despatched to the kidcote on Ouse Bridge. Kidcote is an old Yorkshire word for prison or gaol.

The kidcote on Ouse Bridge was a relatively new prison. The Corporation of York maintained several offices, a toll booth and two gaols (sometimes known as the debtors' prison and the mayor's prison) on and around the area of the bridge. The kidcote had been re-opened in 1574 in one of the final parts of the long running completion of the repairs made to the bridge and buildings above it following the collapse of the previous decade.

Of course, these weren't the only prisons in York. The Church had its own jail, the Peter prison, located next to York Minster. The most important prisoners held in the city were often housed in the prison at York Castle, in an area adjacent to Clifford's Tower (where today you'll find a new English Heritage visitor centre). At various times, there were also a variety of other jails, plus houses of correction, in the city.

In 1576, the then serving Lord Mayor of York was a pewterer called Edmund Richardson. When Lord Mayor Richardson died during his term in office, one of his fellow aldermen, the merchant Ralph Hall, stood in for the remaining months of the mayoral period.

In his will, Mayor Richardson bequeathed his body for burial in the parish church of St Sampson near to the stall where he'd traded his goods. The will also included a number of very Catholic worded clauses and requests. For example, Richardson asked for his soul to be left to God and the saints. Words like these were very much discouraged by the Church and wider authorities.

Edmund Richardson was one of the last few aldermen in

York to write such an openly Catholic will. His passing and some of the events which followed marked the beginning of the changing of the guard in the makeup of the Corporation's aldermen - from Catholic sympathisers to Protestant loyalists.

The next Lord Mayor John Dyneley, however, was definitely a Catholic, although at times and in certain company he probably tried to keep this quiet. During his own term in office, Dyneley's wife was accused of being a recusant. Lady Dyneley just happened to be the sister of the ex-Member of Parliament and wealthy gentleman Edward Besley, who we previously briefly mentioned as having been sent to prison for refusing to go to church.

When Lord Mayor Dyneley was called before the Ecclesiastical High Commission to answer the recusancy charges against his wife, he was given a dressing down for being *"a man who is set to govern a city and cannot govern his own household"*.

In his wife's defence, Dyneley claimed she'd been ill, but he'd be sure to see she attended church services in future. If she was too ill to attend, he added, he would commit to pay regular forfeiture fines on her behalf.

Illness was often a cause which was cited, or perhaps a ready-made excuse, in cases of recusancy. A second alderman and future Lord Mayor Robert Cripling was charged by the same court *"for his wife's like fault"*. After hearing the charges lodged against his own wife, Cripling reassured the Commissioners he'd bring her to the service at the Minster on Sunday *"and thereafter as her health will permit"*.

This same excuse was used by Brian Palmes, a gentleman from Naburn near York, when he appeared in court to face similar changes due to his wife's non-attendance of church services. In the family's defence, Palmes claimed she'd recently been sick. He promised the commissioners he'd pay the fines required on his wife's behalf and invite the vicar of Bishopthorpe into their house to say a special service for his wife. However, it appears the Palmes family had no intention of doing so. Subsequently, they were called back to the court several times to hear further charges regarding their non-attendance.

One York draper George Hall also attended the High Commission on the same day to answer identical charges about his wife's alleged recusancy. In his defence, Hall argued he'd done all he reasonably could to get his wife to church. This included beating her *"now and then"*.

When he was asked to pay a fine, Hall complained that *"he was a poor man and not able to pay"*. A little cheekily, he also added he'd pay the same rate as the one levied against the mayor and the alderman, probably believing they'd both not been punished. The commissioners were having none of it. Ruling against Hall, they instructed he would have to pay fines at the standard rate *"according to the Statute of the Realm"*.

By this time, the Archbishop and court commissioners had begun to lose their patience. They recognised that it was very often the woman of the household who was being charged, when they suspected a whole family of being Catholic. Equally, they disliked the claims of illness which were being heard too often in the court for their liking and were often so difficult to disprove.

Lastly, they began to believe that the fines and forfeitures they had been levying in the majority of recusancy cases simply weren't working. Greater punishments would be needed. From the next set of hearings onwards, York's prisons began to fill up with not just one or two but many more of York's Catholic citizens.

From August 1577, a series of new cases were brought before the Ecclesiastical High Commission as the new approach began to be taken. In one case, the court heard how Anne Weddel *"frequenth not the church, the cause whereof is that her conscience will not serve her thereunto".* The court found Anne guilty and promptly sent her to York Castle prison.

If the Weddell family believed this would be the limit of their punishment, they were quickly proved wrong. The court asked Anne's husband John if he'd instructed his wife to go to church, or whether she'd deceived him. John answered he'd advised her to go to church, but she'd refused to attend. The court wasn't satisfied with John's reply and his failure to keep his wife in order. Much to his surprise, he was committed to the kidcote on Ouse Bridge.

Next up came the case of John and Margaret Clitherow. By this time, Margaret had been part of York's recusant community for around three years. The previous absence of her name and some of the others from the court's records may have been down to the reluctance of the parish churches and Corporation to compile accurate recusancy lists.

However, things were changing. Even the Lord Mayor of York and another alderman had been unable to keep their own wives' names off the lists. Increasingly, recusant Catholics in York could no longer expect to get away with things and go unpunished if they or members of their families refused to attend church services.

The charges made against Margaret Clitherow were read out in court, *"John's wife refuseth service and summons and also to communicate".* The Clitherows received the same punishment as the Weddells. Margaret was despatched to York Castle, while John was sent to the cells in the kidcote on Ouse Bridge. This was to be the first of a series of regular visits to York's courts and prisons for the Clitherows.

A number of further cases followed in a similar fashion. Each ended with the same result. The accused included Peter and Isabel Porter, Ambrose and Anne Cooke, Perceival and Janet Geldard and Thomas and Margaret Tailor. Each of the wives was accused of refusing to attend church services and each was sent to York Castle. Their husbands were committed to Ouse Bridge. Having been brought before the court eighteen months before on similar charges, the Geldards and Porters were repeat offenders.

After three miserable nights in the cells, John Clitherow, John Weddell, Peter Porter, Ambrose Cooke, Perceival Geldard and Thomas Tailor were all brought back before the High Commission. Each was instructed to take out a bond of £20 (a significant sum in those days), and told they had to return before the commissioners in October. They were then released.

The men were forced to return to stand before the High Commission a number of times during the coming months, but their wives remained in prison throughout the autumn and winter. If the commissioners believed this would break the women's resolve, they were wrong. Their spell in the cells served only to strengthen the women's faith. If anything, they became even more committed and even more determined to defy the authorities in future. This was particularly true of Margaret Clitherow.

Not all of the prisoners tried in August 1577 ended up in prison. One of them, Elizabeth Hewett, was also accused of recusancy. Unusually for a woman, her occupation was recorded in the High Commission records. Elizabeth was listed as an *"obstetrix"* or a midwife.

As both a recusant and a midwife, it's very probable Elizabeth Hewett had a close connection to the Vavasours. Spared prison, she was ordered to begin to attend church services. She was also suspended from her midwifery duties until Michaelmas (29 September) unless special permission was provided by the Archbishop. Given his wife was with child at this time, perhaps Archbishop Sandys thought such an exception clause may prove to be useful.

Sometimes, it wasn't just the woman who refused to go to

church and was summonsed to appear in court, particularly if the family could afford it. One York gentleman Edward Tesh of Bishopfields attended the High Commission with his wife Anne alongside him in the dock. Both faced similar accusations of their recusancy. *"He refuseth sermons service and the communion and his wife also"*.

In court, the couple admitted they'd been unable to *"find it in their consciences"* to go to church. The Teshes were offered lodging and conferences at Bishopthorpe to bring them around to the Protestant way of thinking. When they refused this offer, they were threatened with the cells of York Castle. After this, they relented. Anne was allowed to return to their home and have meetings there, while Edward promised to attend special sessions with Church officials at the Archbishop's palace. Perhaps he agreed to this with his fingers and toes crossed. The Teshes went on to become serial recusants. Both later served long prison sentences.

At times, some people refused to attend court hearings or attempted to flee justice by going on the run. When this happened, the courts often hired pursuivants to bring the fugitives to justice. For example, the Ecclesiastical High Commission records show that the court made an agreement with one of the pursuivants, Anthony Durrell. The court documented that Durrell would be paid 3d or 4d for every man, or man and wife, he apprehended in York and 8d a mile (4d each way) for those he'd been forced to travel beyond the city walls to arrest.

In 1577, the Privy Council wrote a letter of complaint to the Corporation, via the Earl of Huntingdon. Once again, the Corporation was accused of a lack of diligence in the prosecution of recusants. Despite the growing number of cases being heard, the Council of the North and Ecclesiastical High Commission remained unimpressed with the Corporation's ability to create full and complete lists of recusants in York.

The Lord Mayor and Corporation officials must have been annoyed. After all, the lists they'd provided had already included the wife of the Lord Mayor and a second alderman. What more could the Ecclesiastical High Commission realistically expect?

During October 1577, Lord Mayor Dyneley found out. He was given just five days to return before the High Commission with an updated and complete list of recusants to be compiled by the Corporation's officers using the records of each individual parish, including full details of *"what hath been done against each"* person listed.

On 29 October, John Dyneley appeared once more before the trio of Archbishop Sandys, Lord President Huntingdon and Dean Hutton. Probably reluctantly, he handed over a longer list of names of potential recusants. After this, he was given another lecture about the need to do his duty and reminded of his wife's disobedience due to her continued non-attendance of church. The Lord Mayor was forced to hand over forty shillings to cover the sixteen Sundays and four holidays since July. Despite the couple's previous promises, Lady Dyneley still hadn't attended a single church service.

The October 1577 list of recusants passed to the Ecclesiastical High Commission makes for fascinating reading. It includes the names of people accused of being absent from York's churches along with additional details of how their cases were being followed up, as written up by the churchwardens of York's parishes.

Some of the entries include either a refusal or an inability to pay fines and details of unsuccessful visits to recusants' houses. The churchwardens at Christs' Church, for example, had made an attempt to question Dorothy Vavasour for *"she cometh not to church"*. The report continued that her husband Thomas was already in prison, but she refused to talk to them and *"keepeth the door closed"*.

In the same parish, George Hall, the man who'd previously defended himself by claiming he'd beaten his wife, admitted to the churchwardens he'd made no further progress on the matter. *"He will submit himself to my Lord Bishop for he cannot get his wife to go to church"*.

Once again illness was often cited as a key reason for non-attendance. The wife of William Cockburn, for example, was said to be *"very sick"*.

The churchwardens of St Sampson's reported that they'd been unable to interview Elizabeth Langton because *"both she and her husband were out... the young folks locked the doors and would not let the churchwardens in"*. Perhaps the children's parents were at home all along, hiding in a corner wishing not to be interviewed.

Some entries also gave the reasons why recusants hadn't paid their fines, often termed as *"distress"*. In St Cuthbert's parish, for example, Helen Williamson had missed all church services since January but her husband John *"hath no goods whereof any distress can be levied"*.

At St Michael le Belfry (the parish church of Guy Fawkes' family next to the Minster), Margaret Tessimond, a saddler's wife, was listed as being absent from church since January. She'd steadfastly refused to permit the churchwardens into her home to take any distress. It must have been a hard life for Margaret Tessimond. If you remember, her husband William was already in prison for trimming the beard off the severed head of the Earl of Northumberland and in a few years time her son would leave St Peter's school to travel abroad to train and become a Catholic priest.

CHAPTER TWENTY-FIVE
Trade and the Merchant Adventurers

After more than a century of creeping decline, finally during the reign of Queen Elizabeth the population and economy of York began to recover. The city's financial records reported positive budget surpluses for each and every year between 1576 and 1583. Although the Queen didn't visit York, over the years there were a number of lavish celebrations. A significant one for example was held in 1581 to celebrate the Earl of Huntingdon's appointment as the Lord Lieutenant of the Northern Counties.

The city's population growth was aided both by the lack of epidemics and increased economic growth. While the establishment of the Ecclesiastical High Commission and the permanent housing of the Council of the North hadn't much helped York's Catholics, both were generating additional valuable revenue for the city.

Another factor behind York's economic recovery was the significant growth in the amount of trade between the city, the rest of England and mainland Europe. York's tradesmen and merchants were increasingly providing and selling goods and services to people across a large area of England. For example, York's craftsmen travelled and sold their wares in markets and at fairs across much of the northern half of the country and sometimes beyond.

York remained an important stopping off point for travellers due to its location as a major crossroads. The Great North Road route linked together London and the Southeast of

England with the Northeast of England and Edinburgh, while the east to west route connected the major port of Hull with the West Riding of Yorkshire and Lancashire. York's inns and alehouses were often seen to be doing excellent business. Even one-off events like the commission to decide the future of Mary Queen of Scots brought in extra visitors and trade to the city.

The number of inns and alehouses in York had increased greatly during Elizabeth's reign. By 1596, sixty-four men and women were licensed to be innkeepers in York. Of the sixty-four inns in the city, forty-six of them were in the central area. In addition, another hundred and three people were licensed as alehouse keepers and eighty-three people were licensed to brew beer. Most of the brewers also had other occupations. The ratio of population to alehouse was estimated to have been around a hundred people to every alehouse. While there were a lot of churches in York, there were even more drinking establishments.

Being an innkeeper had even become a respectable profession. During the time of Henry VII, inn holders had not been allowed to be elected as aldermen. By the second half of Elizabeth's reign, this had changed. Men like Thomas Harrison and Margaret Clitherow's stepfather Henry Maye had managed to reach the pinnacle of the Corporation, while running their inns at the same time.

Imports were important too. The fuel needed for a growing number of homes and industry had traditionally been based upon the felling and burning of timber. As the sixteenth century progressed, peat turf and coal were increasingly being used. These were imported into or passed through York, transported on both the roads and by river. At one stage, the Corporation had even considered buying and running its own dedicated coal mine located elsewhere in the country.

Another factor was the increase in international trade. York's merchants traded with their peers in a growing number of

European countries. The port of Hull, with its access via the Ouse to the river Humber and the North Sea beyond, was crucial. Unfortunately, the merchants of Hull and York often found themselves to be in competition with each other. As a result, their relationships weren't without conflict. More than once, the Earl of Huntingdon had been forced to intervene and mediate to prevent York and Hull's authorities from placing trade embargoes on each other.

Research by Professor Palliser indicates that by 1579 more than sixty of York's merchants were actively trading through the Baltic Sea. Their ships carried outwards commodity items such as cloth and lead from Yorkshire for export to a number of European countries. On their return, they brought with them an increasingly diverse range of imported goods and cargo, including items such as flax, tallow, pitch, tar, animal hides, wine, cereal grains and other foodstuffs.

York's merchants had originally been incorporated as the guild of Mercers of the City of York in 1430. In 1581, they obtained a second royal charter and officially re-incorporated themselves as the Society of Merchant Adventurers of the City of York. The Merchant Adventurers operated from a fine hall in the city centre located between the streets of Fossgate and Piccadilly. Like many of the Tudor buildings in York, you can still visit the hall today.

One man's actions in particular were critical in the work to obtain the new royal charter for York's merchants. William Robinson was one of York's wealthiest residents. During his lifetime, Robinson bought and owned estates and orchards in and around York and at Newby in the North Riding. Having served his time as one of the Sheriffs of York in 1568, he was elected as an alderman in 1579, following the death of Ralph Hall.

Between 1578 and 1590, Robinson was the master of York's Merchant Adventurers. In 1580, he travelled to London, where he successfully lobbied for the granting of the new charter. The deal he secured critically gave York's Merchant Adventurers a lucrative monopoly on all overseas goods brought into the city and into the neighbouring area of the Ainsty, with the only exclusions being salt and fish.

William Robinson went on to serve York as the city's Lord Mayor in two separate terms in 1581 and 1594. He was one of York's Members of Parliament in 1584 and 1589 and sat on several important government committees. For example, one of the committees focused on what should be done about salted fish and herrings, topics which several of York's merchants would have been very interested in.

When Robinson died in 1616 at the ripe old age (for Tudor times) of eighty-two, he left behind a large estate in his will. This included several donations to benefit the causes he'd supported during his life. A not insignificant sum of £80 was passed to the Corporation to support others in York who wanted to set up their own business. A further £40 was bequeathed to the Merchant Adventurers, with instructions the money should be loaned out interest free to the city's young merchants.

CHAPTER TWENTY-SIX
Poverty in Tudor York

As is so often the case, the growing wealth and prosperity in the city wasn't shared out equally for the benefit of all of its citizens. In Tudor York, the poor and the wealthy often lived together in close proximity to each other within the city walls. In times gone by, the Church had played a major role in the support of the poor, but this had become much more difficult since the dissolution of the monasteries and the other religious houses. In York, important institutions such as St Leonard's Hospital and St Mary's Abbey which had previously provided welfare services were now all closed.

Throughout the Tudor period, national laws were enacted to address poverty and issues such as begging. Collectively, these are often referred to as the Tudor poor laws. Equally, local policies were also set. At times the Corporation of York acted ahead of national measures, while sometimes it responded to them.

Support for the needy in Tudor England was based very much upon a carrot and stick approach. Specific policies were designed to provide relief for the poor, while others were designed to penalise. A new law set out by Parliament in 1572 was typical of this approach. The Act for the Punishment of Vagabonds and the Relief of the Poor and Impotent categorised the poor into those who were deserving of support and those who should be punished.

The new law included a long and definitive list of people

who should be classified as *"rogues, vagabonds or sturdy beggars"* and thus were eligible to suffer punishment. The scope of the definition was surprisingly wide. Those included on the list varied from unlicensed legal professionals and university students to fraudsters, travelling entertainers, released felons and people who refused to work for *"reasonable wages"*. Of course, what could be considered *"reasonable"* was very subjective.

The full list comprises of legal *"proctors and procurators"* who practiced without *"sufficient authority"*, *"other idle people... using subtle, crafty and unlawful games"*, people who feigned knowledge in *"physiognomy, palmistry or other abused sciences"*, *"persons being mighty in body... not having land or master... and can give no reckoning how he or she doth lawfully get his or her living"*, fencers, bear keepers, actors and minstrels *"not belonging to... an honourable person"*, jugglers, pedlars and tinkers who didn't have a proper licence, *"all common labourers of able body... loitering and refusing to work for such reasonable wages"*, counterfeiters, Oxford or Cambridge scholars who were found begging without a licence, unlicensed sailors while on land and released prisoners found to be begging.

The act ordered that anyone who fell into this definition over the age of fourteen who was found to be begging or *"taken vagrant, wandering and mis-ordering themselves"* could be brought before the justices of the peace or other local legal officers and sent to gaol. Once tried, if found guilty, they would be *"grievously whipped and burnt through the gristle of the right ear with a hot iron"* to mark them down as a rogue.

In terms of the carrot, the act transferred civil responsibility for the poor from the Church to the local authorities. *"Aged, impotent and poor people"* were to be provided *"convenient habitations and abiding places throughout the realm to settle themselves upon, to the end that they nor any of them should beg or wander about"*.

"Mayors, sheriffs, bailiffs and other officers" in York and elsewhere were instructed to *"make diligent search and inquiry"* to identify deserving paupers within each of their parishes.

All *"aged, impotent and poor people"* identified were then to be logged in a new register, and a new tax created and administered at a local level to raise funds to support them. Anyone so identified who refused to be housed and supported in this manner could be considered and punished as a *"rogue or vagabond"*.

In advance of the 1572 law, the Corporation had already acted. Earlier on during Elizabeth's reign in 1561 the Corporation had created a system of rates to fund enhanced support for some of the poorest people in the city. The primary aim of this move was to reduce the level of begging on the city's streets, which had continued to be a problem despite the growing economy.

By 1566, the Corporation had created an initial register to identify both those who should be supported and those who should be punished, although the scope wasn't as wide as identified in the new act. In 1570, around ninety people were given a licence to beg in York.

A second new law followed in 1576. The Act for the Setting of the Poor to Work and for the Avoiding of Idleness focused on providing work for the able-bodied poor. It included instructions that each local authority should create a *"stock of wool, hemp, flax, iron or other stuff"* which was to be distributed amongst the poor for them to work on. Finished goods were then to be sold and the revenue generated used to fund more supplies.

Once again, York was ahead of its time. Weaving houses for the poor had already been created in St Anthony's Hall in 1567 and at St George's Chapel in 1569 where *"the city wool is, then and there to be proved by the aldermen, wardens and Twenty-Four."*

A local tradesman volunteered or was assigned to provide guidance, so the poor could work, *"with the advice of Roger Ligle, clothier, what they can do; and such of them as can do ought, or are meet to learn to have wool delivered them by discretion of such as have charge thereof to work, and the said Roger to do his diligence to instruct such of the said poor as he shall perceive not perfect"*.

In 1574, the Corporation went a step further by creating dedicated space in each of St Thomas's, the Merchants' Hall and St Anthony's Hall. The locations were used to provide a roof over the heads of fifty *"impotent, poor and lame"* people in York and to give them a place to work in. A steady supply of hemp and linen was also provided by the city's authorities.

The stick in the 1576 act was that any persons who refused to work, or be supported as described above, could be committed instead to a *"house of correction"*. Once there, they would be forced to carry out manual labour as directed by the local authority. As instructed in the 1576 act, the Corporation opened houses of correction for those who refused to work. The first of these was located in St George's Chapel. Anyone sufficiently unfortunate to be sent there would effectively be held prisoner by the city and forced to carry out hard labour.

So many people in York fell into this category that St George's was soon full and extra capacity had to be provided. An additional house of correction was temporarily created at Fishergate Bar in 1584, before this was replaced in 1586 by the lower floor of St Anthony's. Remarkably, this part of St Anthony's Hall continued to be used as a house of correction in York until the nineteenth century.

The treatment of people in Tudor York classified as *"rogues, vagabonds or sturdy beggars"* often depended upon where they'd originally come from. Anyone local to York who refused to work would be treated by the Corporation and the courts as detailed above, incarcerated and put to work.

The situation for immigrant paupers was different. In 1577, twenty-one paupers in York were identified as being from outside the city. Along with their families they were expelled from York and told to go back to their place of origin. While most of the families hailed from the local surrounding countryside, villages and market towns, one family had travelled to York from Hull. Another had come from Richmond in Yorkshire. A third family had come from as far afield as Norwich. In a later case, one vagrant was whipped according to the law, thrown out through the city gates and instructed to return to Hampshire.

In 1587, the Corporation created a new three-way classification of the most unfortunate people in the city. Once again, this distinguished between those who the authorities considered warranted support and those who should be punished.

The first category encompassed people who, due to their age or infirmity, were adjudged to be in genuine need of assistance. Individuals in this group were paid through their parish a minimum amount of three and halfpence a day to enable their survival. This amount was chosen as it was estimated that *"under which sum a poor creature cannot live"*.

Citizens included in the second group were those who were classified as being fit and able to work but through no fault of their own remained unemployed. Rather than provide these people with a hand-out, the Corporation developed instead a rather innovative and embryonic job creation scheme. Aldermen, councillors and other officials were offered one or more of these unemployed people to work for them. In exchange, the unemployed were provided with subsistence payments.

The third and final category included those who were viewed as being able-bodied but unwilling to work. Such people were viewed extremely dimly by the authorities and as described above, were placed in one of the houses of correction or forcibly expelled from the city.

We'll complete this chapter by examining the at times contrasting treatment of the poor in late Elizabethan York depending on where they came from. We'll start with the very sad story of Margaret Sheles, a woman described in the records as *"a notorious vagabond"*. Having *"loitered within and about the city of York"* for around a decade, Sheles had already been whipped, burned through the ear and sent away multiple times, but probably due to desperation and having nowhere else to go she kept on returning.

One York couple were so exasperated by her continued presence, they complained to the Northern Ecclesiastical High Commission with a view to them meting out further punishment to the unfortunate woman. This was a tricky issue. The possible penalties for repeat offenders included capital punishment. The commissioners decided to wash their hands of the matter and passed responsibility for her case onto the local jurisdiction of the Corporation of York. The commissioners made a request to the Corporation to deliver *"such punishment... as you think shall restrain her access thereafter"*. After this, it's not clear if Margaret Sheles ever returned to York again.

The treatment given to those consigned to hard labour and vagabonds from outside York, such as Margaret Sheles, contrasts with the more compassionate approach, which was sometimes demonstrated by York's authorities, particularly to their own.

Near to the end of Queen Elizabeth's reign, a widow called Atkinson (we don't know her first name) was found to be homeless in Micklegate. Records show she was identified as caring for *"diverse small children"*. Following a brief investigation, the Corporation recognised that the family were in such dire straits that they would likely be *"starving this next winter"*.

The local parish wardens in Micklegate were instructed to find a home for Widow Atkinson along with her children. However, the problem of poverty continued to blight many in York until the final days of the Tudor dynasty and well beyond.

CHAPTER TWENTY-SEVEN
Crime and Punishment

With poverty still affecting some sections of York's population, many people struggled to make ends meet. With the rich and the desperate living so close together, money lending was rife. In 1571, a new national law was enacted by Parliament. This set the maximum rate of interest which could be levied on loans at ten per cent. However, many York wealthy merchants, including a fair number of Corporation officials, often continued to charge significantly higher rates than this.

This was an area where the Archbishop of York Edwin Sandys frequently clashed with many of York's wealthiest citizens throughout his term of office. In 1577, during his very first sermon in the city, he started as he meant to go on. Raging from the pulpit in the Minster, Archbishop Sandys denounced the evils of usury and all those who practiced it, condemning the rich for lending money in a way which took advantage of those who were much less fortunate than themselves.

During many of his later sermons, Sandys returned to the same topic. One was titled *"Owe nothing to any man"*. Sandys took an extremely dim view of anyone he considered to be a usurer or money lender, saying, *"his own soul is vile, nothing is precious but only money"*.

In another sermon, the Archbishop quoted Jesus as saying, *"Lend, looking for nothing thereby: and your reward shall be much: you shall be the sons of the Most High"*.

After this, he went on to preach, *"So that these over-*

payments, the usury which hath spoiled and eaten up many, the canker of the commonwealth, is utterly both forbidden to man, and abhorred of God".

During his eleventh major sermon in York, Sandys didn't mince his words at all when he warned what would happen to the money lenders in the city following their death. God, he preached, would *"...exclude thee out of his kingdom... and hurl thee into hell, where thy evil gotten money can neither redeem nor help thee. A just reward for thy unjust usury!"*

With this sort of rhetoric, it's little wonder the Archbishop earned himself the nickname of *"hammer of the usurers"*. In one of his by now regular letters to William Cecil, Sandys complained that usury was being practiced in York *"more than anywhere else in the world... its hath eaten up the poor and spoiled the gentlemen"*.

Unlike many of his peers though, Archbishop Sandys was in a position where he was able to back up his angry words about usury with actions. After all, he was the leader of the Ecclesiastical High Commission. Although this court had been established primarily to drive religious uniformity, Sandys made a decision to utilise it as a vehicle for prosecuting the *"vile"* souls who lent money to and earned immoral interest from the city's poor. In this way, he was keen to ensure York's money lenders would suffer on Earth even before they were later *"hurled into hell"* following their deaths.

In one case, the Ecclesiastical court *"called before them seven usurers... and upon their confession and proof admitted of great and excessive usury, acknowledged the same and submitted themselves to order; which was that they should enter into recognisance of one thousand marks apiece never to commit the like and to make restitution to the party aggrieved of that which they had received more than the principal."*

As part of their punishment, the seven men who'd been

found guilty of usury were forced to forfeit all the interest they'd charged, rather than just the profits they'd made above the legal rate of ten per cent. The judgement was welcomed by York's poorest citizens who'd been forced to borrow from their wealthier neighbours, but it wasn't universally popular. Many of York's merchants were none too pleased with Edwin Sandys and he was soon reminded he'd made some dangerous enemies.

A second case was held two weeks later. A further twenty men were brought to court. Part way through the first session, there was a dramatic intervention in the courtroom from the Dean of York Matthew Hutton.

"...the Dean of York of purpose to hinder this good and lawful proceeding... saying 'We must beware how we deal in this matter of usury. For my part I dissent from these proceedings and mislike of them; so will clear my hands of it: for many things are termed usury in the civil law which are not usury by the word of God'".

Archbishop Sandys was furious about the court being interrupted in this way, but Dean Hutton wouldn't back down. When Hutton refused to support the men's prosecution, the proceedings were halted for the day. Sandys despatched the accused to the cells of York Castle prison. A day later the prisoners were freed. This followed an order which had been made by the Council of the North.

Dean Hutton may have well teamed up with his long-term ally the Earl of Huntingdon to foil Sandys' plans. Equally, it's possible the Council of the North determined the Archbishop was simply overstepping the mark. Part of the Council's role, after all, was to uphold the Queen's laws in the North of England. While Sandys had argued the men could charge no interest at all, the law begged to differ. Since 1571, interest repayments could be levied, up to but no more than the maximum legal rate of ten per cent.

However, the Archbishop wasn't finished. New cases were heard. Four new usurers were brought to court, including one of York's Sheriffs William Gibson. The men all admitted that they had made loans, but these hadn't yet been repaid. The court instructed they should not be paid any interest and the men were asked to swear to not commit usury in future.

Another three men were ordered to repay all of the interest they'd received from their debtors. The principal of their loans was also to be sacrificed to make good the costs of the court.

Other men were also accused, but the next group of merchants refused to bow down to the authority of the court. One of their number, James Mudd, claimed the trial had only been created for *"no other cause but to get the lawyers or some of them money"*. Sandys lost his temper at this point. He sent Mudd and all the other merchants in the dock to York Castle prison.

In this matter, as in others, Archbishop Sandys wasn't averse to upsetting the Earl of Huntingdon. To the Earl's dismay, the Ecclesiastical Commission summonsed one of his own employees, Robert Morley, to attend the court accused of usury. Understanding the statute of 1571, Morley refused to hear the charges made against him, unless he was allowed to have legal representation in court. For the same reason, another man Richard Scott refused to accept the jurisdiction of the court to try him. Both were sent to York Castle prison, but their release was soon ordered by the Earl of Huntingdon.

If Edwin Sandys didn't fully get his own way in preventing all interest payments in York, it was for two reasons. Although they were often allies on religious matters, he'd made notable enemies of the Dean of York and the Earl of Huntingdon on domestic affairs. Secondly, the civil law of the land was against him. Although Sandys argued all interest payments were evil, immoral and should not be allowed, the 1571 statute disagreed. Under the Queen's law, money lenders were legally allowed to make loans and permitted to charge a rate of interest up to ten per cent.

However, the Archbishop's actions did have a positive effect. The charging of high interest rates in York had been rife. In his sermons, Sandys had quoted rates of thirty per cent and above. A number of York's merchants who'd been forced to pay back the interest they'd earned had also been forced to swear oaths in court promising they'd no longer *"directly or indirectly commit the vile and detestable crime of usury"*.

Others had been warned off too. If Archbishop Sandys didn't save all of York's less well-off people from this practice, at least he reduced the costs of lending for many of them and they were grateful for it.

#

In addition to having many prisons, Tudor York also housed a variety of different courts of law. These varied from hearings with regional jurisdiction, such as those run by the Ecclesiastical High Commission and Council of the North, to local courts administered by Corporation officials such as the Sheriffs and the Lord Mayor. An additional court of some importance also sat in York twice during the year in Lent and in August. This was the travelling assizes court where the judges heard some of the more serious cases, such as counterfeiting, horse theft, murder and treason. While decisions in most of the courts were made directly by commissioners or officials acting as justices of the peace, others including the assizes court operated a jury system.

Depending on the particular court and the offence, citizens found guilty could face various punishments. These varied from verbal admonishments to fines and imprisonment in one of York's many prisons. One of York's more common misdemeanours was the failure to pay bills or repay loans. So many people in York fell foul of this that one of the Corporation of York's kidcotes on Ouse Bridge was often referred to as the debtors' prison,

Perhaps this was just one of the reasons why Archbishop Sandys was so angry about money lending. We should remember though that the Archbishop wasn't averse to imprisoning people himself, whether for usury, or more frequently as time went by for religious reasons. We'll return to some of the most serious court cases related to religion shortly.

Of course, punishment in Elizabethan York didn't stop at imprisonment. As we've seen, convicted vagabonds could be whipped and a hot iron run through their ears to mark them for life. Corporal punishment and use of the stocks was also meted out for many other crimes, in line with the statue book.

The ultimate sanction though was execution. Capital punishment could be ordered for a relatively wide range of crimes if they were considered to be of a serious nature. Unfortunately in Tudor York, this was all too often the case. The city operated major gallows at the Knavesmire in an area next to where York racecourse is today. Executions were also held at St Leonard's Green Dyke outside Walmgate Bar and occasionally at other locations. For example, the Earl of Northumberland was beheaded on the Pavement in the centre of the city while Thomas Wilson who'd stabbed Archbishop Grindal was hanged in the grounds of St Mary's Abbey.

As York was a regional centre of jurisdiction, many of the criminals tried or executed there came from areas outside the city. In 1581, James Richardson was found guilty of the murder of Thomas Miller in Knaresborough and of stealing £20 of silver coins, He was hanged at St Leonard's Green. In 1583, Peter Clark was hanged at St Leonard's Green for killing Hannah Thompson in Pocklington. During the same year, Rinnion Foster of York suffered the same fate after being found guilty of the rape of Mary Thompson and horse theft.

A number of cases being heard in York's law courts during

the latter part of the sixteenth century referred to the crimes of coining and the counterfeiting of currency. Coining related to the illegal practice of filing down and/or melting coins for recasting or wider use. The victims of these crimes were sometimes the better off members of society. As such, it was taken very seriously.

Anyone found guilty of the *"offences of clipping, rounding, washing and filing, for wicked lucre or gain's sake"* would be adjudged to be committing treason. In 1576, a further Parliamentary act was passed which increased the scope and definition of the crime to: *"Persons... by any ways, arts or means whatsoever, impair, diminish, falsify, scale or lighten the proper monies or coins of the realm... shall be taken, held and adjudged to be treason"*. Any co-conspirators judged as having helped, aided or abetted others in these practices could also be executed for treason.

Judging by the various court records, counterfeiting and coining were serious problems in York. A number of people were arrested, tried and executed for these crimes. In 1575, Frederick Gottfried and Thomas Conrad were hanged on St Leonard's Green for coining guineas in the Thursday market in York. Their bodies were later buried in St Giles's Churchard in Gillygate.

A year later, Edward de Satre and Sarah Houslay were found guilty of possessing forged promissory notes of the value of 50 guineas. They were hanged at the Knavesmire and their bodies were buried behind York Castle walls, near to the river Foss. In 1582, when George Foster of Tadcaster was hanged for coining at the Knavesmire, a large crowd had assembled to watch.

Three years later, George de Kirwan and Thomas de Alasco were both found guilty of coining guineas at the house of the silversmith Simon Pontius in Jubbergate (this was previously where some of York's Jewish community had lived). The men were drawn to the Knavesmire on a sledge and executed. The records don't describe what the silversmith's involvement was, nor what happened to him.

In 1588, Andrew Turner was found guilty of coining. His subsequent execution took place at St Leonard's Green. Three men from York (William de Allestry, Robert de Hammond and Thomas de Allix) came before the courts in 1595. They were each found guilty of coining and paying with *"bad money"*. The trio were executed on the same day at the Knavesmire. Afterwards, their bodies were buried in St. George's Churchyard next to the Fishergate postern.

There were many other cases of coining and counterfeiting but I think you get the point. Men and sometimes women were regularly being executed in Tudor York for crimes such as murder but also for financial crimes. The 1580's, however, saw a new set of executions take place in York. Those who lost their lives at the hands of the state were also accused of treason, though many of them believed they'd done nothing wrong other than fall foul of an unjust set of laws relating to religion.

CHAPTER TWENTY-EIGHT
Priests and Executions

In 1579, Robert Cripling was elected as the new Lord Mayor of York. Two years earlier he'd been brought before the Ecclesiastical High Commission to answer for his wife's non-attendance of church services. Cripling and his fellow alderman John Dyneley were key members of the Corporation's old guard of York's merchants, men who maintained sympathy for and allegiance to the Catholic faith.

In the early months of Cripling's term in office, acting under his instructions the Corporation of York suspended the prosecution of recusants in the civil courts in the city. The Earl of Huntingdon was outraged and reacted angrily at the Corporation's disregard for the law and his own authority. He issued orders that Mayor Cripling was to be arrested and placed in a cell inside York Castle prison.

The pressure from the Council of the North on the Corporation was relentless. At the end of his term of office, the aldermen were compelled to disenfranchise Robert Cripling from the Corporation altogether. The charges made against him included being absent from his duties (although being present would have been a challenge while he'd been held in prison), uttering a string of *"unseemly and foul words"* against Protestant clergymen in York and failing in his legal duties to prosecute the city's recusants.

Although Cripling was forced to resign from his position as one of the Corporation's aldermen (a role which was usually held for life), the authorities hadn't quite finished with him. In November 1580, the ex-Lord Mayor and his wife Lady Cripling were ordered to stand once more before the Ecclesiastical High Commission to face charges of recusancy. The couple were found guilty and ordered to take out a substantial bond.

By stating *"Mr Cripling has conformed completely"*, the court records appeared to indicate that the former Lord Mayor and his wife had begun to toe the line. However, once they were out of the public eye, Robert and Lady Cripling continued to devote themselves to the Catholic faith. Over the next few years, they were frequently forced to return to the courts of the High Commission.

Around the same time, York's other Catholic-leaning ex-Lord Mayor John Dyneley died. His widow was also a long-standing recusant. After her husband's death, she left York and re-married another Catholic.

The early 1580s saw a major change in the make-up of York's aldermen. Robert Cripling had been forced to leave the Corporation by the Council of the North. John Dyneley had died. In 1581, a third alderman known to have Catholic sympathies, William Alleyn, resigned from his position.

Although he may also have been under pressure from the Council of the North, Alleyn had previously fallen out with several of his fellow aldermen. He decided to move away and live outside York. As aldermen were expected to reside within the city's walls, Alleyn was instructed by his colleagues to return or resign. He opted for the latter.

Thus three out of the thirteen aldermen, all with clear Catholic leanings, had left the Corporation within a matter of months. More were to follow. Despite the lack of any major epidemic or illness, three additional aldermen (Thomas Appleyard, John Beane and Richard Calom) all died between 1580 and 1581. In addition, York's official recorder William

Bernard passed away around the same time. He was replaced by Sir William Hildyard, who became a Member of Parliament for the city in 1586.

Half a dozen replacement aldermen now had to be elected in a relatively short space of time. All needed to be sworn into office. Having witnessed the treatment meted out to Catholic sympathisers like Cripling and Dyneley and under pressure from the Council of the North and the Church, the remaining aldermen had a decision to make. While reviewing which members of the council of the Twenty-Four were most suitable for promotion, should they select purely on merit or favour candidates of a more obviously loyal Protestant persuasion? It appears, in general, the aldermen favoured the latter option.

While the odd embarrassing alderman's relative did pop up from time to time in the recusancy courts in the coming years, the lingering allegiance to the old religion in the Corporation's higher echelons was over. The 1580s saw a number of loyalist Protestants, including Henry Maye (Margaret Clitherow's stepfather), elected as aldermen. The relationship between the Corporation of York and the Council of the North began to thaw.

In 1580-81, forty-five new names were added to York's recusancy lists. Facing further punishment, a number of the city's recusants opted to conform. Discarding their Catholicism, they began to attend the Protestant Church of England.

This wasn't always the case. Many of York's remaining recusants had already served long prison sentences together. While inside their cells, they'd had little else to talk and think about other than theology and their increasing devotion to the Catholic faith. York's gaols had become a place where prisoners of conscience confided with people of like minds. Perhaps the majority of York's religious prisoners found their convictions were strengthening during their time inside the prisons rather than weakening. In modern terminology, we might consider some of them as having been radicalised.

Archbishop Sandys, Dean Hutton and many other senior churchmen considered the convicted Catholic prisoners as a captive audience for conversion to their own faith. The Archbishop, the Dean of York and a plethora of other Protestant clergymen visited the cells and preached long sermons to York's recusants in an effort to convince them of the error of their ways.

Sometimes, the prisoners were challenged to dispute what they'd heard in the belief this would aid their conversion. One of the prisoners, Thomas Mudd a former monk, warmed to the argument. He made such a strong case against the Archbishop that Edwin Sandys struggled to refute it. The Archbishop became furious and threatened to have him *"crushed and bruised"*. Seemingly unable to counter Mudd's arguments, Sandys soon had the prisoner transferred to the worse conditions of Hull prison, where Mudd promptly fell ill.

During 1581 and in 1582, York began to see an influx of a new breed of Catholic priests. Some of these men had originally come from Yorkshire and some had not. All had previously left England, trained on the continent at one of the new *"English colleges"* and joined the Catholic priesthood. They were then instructed to return to their homeland, effectively as undercover missionary priests. Their task was to spread the word of Catholic theology to the faithful and anyone else who might be willing to convert.

It was an extremely dangerous thing to do. Catholic priests were viewed by the English authorities as traitors to the crown and the country. A series of new laws were enacted. Each brought increasing levels of punishment against the priests. By the 1580's, the new laws had changed to consider priests as traitors. Treason, of course, was a capital crime.

The priests came to England undercover, wearing disguises and often using aliases. The men regularly moved around local circuits, living for short periods of time in the homes of different Catholic households, including a number in York, before moving on. Sometimes they pretended they were school masters and lived with a family for a longer period. They preached, held secret Catholic masses, heard confession and provided other religious services.

In July 1582, a group of undercover priests planned to hold a meeting with York's Catholic community. With so many Catholics incarcerated inside York Castle, rather amazingly they decided to hold their conference there. In total, four priests attended the meeting. These were Fathers Thomas Bell, William Hart, William Lacy and Anthony Tyrrell.

The four fathers gained entry to York Castle, most likely by bribing the guards and warders. Once inside, they remained in the prison for several hours. The priests gave sermons, heard Mass, listened to and absolved confessions, and read prayers without any interruption or interference. Their luck however couldn't last forever. Finally, once they became aware of what was going on inside their own gaol, the authorities moved in.

Sensing the danger, the four fathers attempted to make an escape. Father Hart later reported what happened next. He hauled himself up over a high wall and pushed his way through a moat, with the water at one stage reaching his chin. Once he'd waded to the other side, soaked to the skin, he made a break for freedom through York's dark streets. Given shelter by one of York's Catholic families, Father Hart got away, as did Fathers Bell and Tyrrell.

In the end, only one out of the four priests, Father William Lacy, was apprehended. Father Lacy was placed inside a cell with another priest, Father Richard Kirkman, who'd also recently been arrested. The two men were eventually brought before the assizes court and tried for offences related to the 1581 Disobedience Act, which had been designed to deter and punish

Catholic priests from entering the country.

In the bloody reign of Queen Mary I, not a single execution on religious grounds had taken place in York. Unfortunately, this was not to be the case under Mary's half-sister Elizabeth I. On 22 August 1582, William Lacy and Richard Kirkman were transported from York Castle prison to York's own Tyburn, the Knavesmire, where they were publicly executed.

During the same month, another Catholic priest was arrested in York. James Thompson was a local man who'd only left his home city a year earlier. Having travelled to France and been ordained as a priest, he'd returned to England and come back to York. Father Thompson was arrested celebrating Mass in the home of a blacksmith William Branton in the parish of St Michel le Belfrey, near to York Minster. Under questioning from the Council of the North, he confessed to being a Catholic seminary priest.

Following his arrest, Father Thompson was shackled in irons and imprisoned. For a while he paid to be held in a more comfortable private prison in the city. When his money ran out, he was placed in York Castle. In November 1582, the Council of the North tried him and found him guilty of treason. A few days later he was transported to the Knavesmire. Before his death, Father Thompson stressed despite his Catholicism he remained loyal to both England and the Queen. For this reason perhaps, he wasn't hanged, drawn and quartered like most of the other priests. However, he was still hanged as a traitor.

James Thompson wasn't the only young Catholic man who'd left York to train to become a priest on the continent, although many of them didn't return to their local area where they might so easily be recognised. A number of Guy Fawkes' former peers from St Peter's School, for example, left the city to join the Catholic priesthood. Such men included Edward Oldcorne, Oswald Tessimond and Robert Middleton.

Other men who left York for a similar reason included the two pairs of brothers Thomas and William Wright and Richard and Thomas Cowling. Henry Clitherow, the eldest child of John and Margaret Clitherow, also made the same journey but unlike most of the others he never returned to England.

Despite the brutal treatment and executions being meted out to many of their friends and colleagues, the remaining Catholic priests in York didn't flee away from the city or abandon their flock. For example, following the dramatic escape from the Catholic meeting at York Castle prison, Father Hart continued to operate as an undercover priest in York for some time. He was hidden by a series of families in various secret rooms and continued to administer Mass and hear confession for them, including for people such as Dorothy Vavasour and Margaret Clitherow.

Christmas was a busy time of year for the priests. On Christmas Day in 1582, Father Hart was asked to say Mass in the family home of William Hutton (who very probably was not related to the arch anti-Catholic Dean of York Matthew Hutton).

William wasn't at home at this time, as he was already serving a sentence in prison for recusancy. After a fine meal with the man's family, Father Hart became tired and fell asleep. On Christmas night, he was roused from his slumber by the sounds of pursuivants who'd come to arrest him. Father Hart's location and his true identity had been betrayed to the authorities by an informer. It's believed the man had previously been a Catholic who had converted to the Protestant faith.

Father Hart was taken to the Council of the North and questioned by the Lord President the Earl of Huntingdon, himself. After his interrogation, the priest was held in custody and informed he would be tried by the travelling assizes court when it next sat in York during Lent. Following three long and very cold months in jail, the assizes court found Father Hart to be guilty of treason, and he was executed in March 1583.

Despite their losses, the priests kept on coming. Richard Kirkeld had left Durham to train as a priest. When he returned to England, he came to York, said Mass and heard confession for many Catholics. Once again, they included Margaret Clitherow. Rather bravely or foolishly depending upon your point of view, Father Kirkeld visited a Catholic prisoner being held in the kidcote on Ouse Bridge. Despite his disguise of layman's apparel, he was suspected of being a priest and arrested.

When they searched him, the Sheriffs' men discovered two keys inside Father Kirkeld's clothing. These were identified as having been made locally in a workshop in York. The keys were taken to William Hutton's house (the place where Father Hart had been arrested on Christmas night) and used to open a wooden trunk which was discovered to be packed full of illegal Catholic books. The books were carried over to the Pavement for all to see and very publicly burned in the street.

In addition to the usual charges of being a Catholic priest and a traitor, Father Kirkeld was also accused of attempting to convert one or more of the Queen's subjects to the Catholic Church. The father was tried by the Council of the North's Quarterly Sessions court in May 1583 and found guilty. A day after his trial, he was put to death.

CHAPTER TWENTY-NINE
Catholic Martyrdom

The brutal executions of William Lacy, Richard Kirkman, William Hart and Richard Kirkeld for simply being Catholic priests and/or attempting to convert people to Catholicism shines a light onto the darker aspects of life in Elizabethan York. The 1580's must have been a frightening time to be a Catholic in the city. The constant pressure being placed upon them forced some of York's Catholic recusants to conform.

For example, a number of members of the families of York's butchers were brought before the Ecclesiastical High Commission in October 1580. The results of their cases were as follows:

- *"Chris Rayne, butcher of York, and wife Margaret – both to certify conformity by 17 January"*
- *"Roger Spence, butcher of York, brought in Millicent, wife of William Calvert, for whose appearance he was surety – she proved she was continuing her conformity, so dismissed"*
- *"Michael Mudd, butcher of York, and wife Ellen – she is sick; he took bond they would both conform and certify"*
- *"Stephen Preston, butcher of York, and wife Jane – took bond to conform themselves and certify"*

The other recusancy cases in York in 1580 provide a fascinating glimpse of the guilds and trades of Tudor York. In addition to butchers, those called before the courts that month included gentlemen, merchants, an apothecary, an armourer, a baker, a cord-wainer (shoemaker), a currier (leather worker), a pewterer, a tanner, a tapster (weaver), multiple tailors and, of course, many of their wives.

Although some of the butchers' families and others had promised to conform, many later found themselves called once again before the courts after refusing to do so or having subsequently reverted to their old ways. Another of York's butchers John Clitherow also found himself back in front of the court during the same month with his wife Margaret. When she flatly refused to promise to conform and go to church, she was sent to serve her second sentence in York Castle prison.

Margaret Clitherow was subsequently released on licence for a short period in April 1581. This was to allow her to give birth to the couple's third child. After returning to prison and completing her sentence, she was released. However, she was soon back in court. In March 1583, Margaret Clitherow was sentenced to serve a further ten months inside York Castle.

Her husband John watched on as his wife returned to prison. The impact on his family life and business must have been significant. His wife and the mother of their young children was often not at their home in the Shambles for months on end. Down the years. he'd had to pay out many hefty fines for his wife's recusancy.

Having remained a Protestant, John Clitherow regularly attended church services. At times, he'd even been a church warden in the family's parish church of Christ's Church or the Church of the Holy Trinity in King's Square. The church no longer exists, but there is an inscription on the paving stones there to mark where it once stood.

Another couple constantly in trouble for their recusancy was Thomas and Dorothy Vavasour. With her husband in prison, Dorothy had become one of the Catholics in York who sheltered Catholic priests and allowed them to live and say Mass in secret rooms in their own house.

In late 1581, the authorities raided the Vavasours' house while an elderly priest was officiating Mass. The raid was supported by a group of Corporation aldermen, including the newly elected Henry Maye. Dorothy's case was brought before the Quarterly Sessions court. The priest, William Wilkinson, was sent to gaol, while Dorothy was fined a hundred marks and sent to the kidcote on Ouse Bridge to serve a long spell in prison.

In May 1585, while his wife was still incarcerated in York, Dorothy Vavasour's husband, the medical doctor Thomas Vavasour who'd been ill for some time, died in his prison cell in Hull. In the same year, two other Catholics, John Ackbridge and Stephen Hemsworth, also died while serving jail sentences in York.

When Margaret Clitherow was released from prison, she too began to host Catholic priests, including both Fathers Hart and Kirkeld who were subsequently arrested and executed. In 1584, two new undercover Catholic priests arrived in York. Both needed Catholic families to house and shelter them and both sometimes stayed in secret rooms inside and near to John and Margaret's Clitherow's house and butcher's shop in the Shambles in the centre of York.

Father Francis Ingleby was the son of Sir William Ingleby of Ripley Castle in Yorkshire. Francis's sister Jane was married to George Wintour of Worcestershire. Two decades later, Jane's sons Thomas and Robert Wintour would go on to become Gunpowder Plotters alongside Guy Fawkes and the Wright brothers. The second priest Father John Mush also hailed from Yorkshire.

By this time, Margaret Clitherow was playing a very dangerous game. A new law had been enacted in 1585 which made even helping or harbouring a Catholic priest a capital crime. In November 1585, Marmaduke Bowes, a Catholic sympathiser, was arrested for aiding a priest called Father Hugh Taylor. According to one description of the events, Bowes had been harbouring Father Taylor in his house. However, a second report claims Bowes was arrested for simply *"having given Taylor a cup of beer at his door"*.

Hugh Taylor had been arrested separately, tried by the Council of the North and condemned to death. In November 1585, he was the first priest to be executed under the new Parliamentary act *"Against Jesuits, Seminary Priests and Such Other Like Disobedient Persons"*.

Shortly afterwards, Marmaduke Bowes was called before the court, accused of aiding Father Taylor. Twenty-four hours following the execution of Father Taylor, Bowes was also hanged, drawn and quartered in York. Upon his death, he became the first lay person in England and Wales to be executed under the new statute.

A few months later in February 1586, there was a new Lord Mayor in York. Henry Maye's rise to prominence represents a remarkable rags to riches story. Despite coming from a humble background in the south of England, Maye had worked hard and used his wife Jane's wealth and social connections to climb the Corporation of York's ladder to its very pinnacle.

Margaret Clitherow's mother Jane Maye (previously Middleton) died in 1585. This was only a few months before her husband Henry Maye became Lord Mayor. Within days of his elevation, Henry Maye married again. His second wife Anne Thomson was a much younger woman. The only blight on his life appeared to be his recusant stepdaughter, Margaret Clitherow.

To cut a long and fascinating story short, in March 1586 only a month after Henry Maye had become Lord Mayor, the Clitherows' house was raided. Their premises were searched by an official party of pursuivants led by the two Sheriffs of York, the senior man Sheriff Roland Fawcett and his colleague Sheriff William Gibson. The second sheriff was one of the men who'd been taken to court by Archbishop Sandys for money lending.

Although no priests were found in the house, Catholic items were discovered hidden away in a secret chamber. Margaret was arrested. A week later she was placed on trial at the York Lent assizes court. She was accused of harbouring Fathers Francis Ingleby and John Mush, who'd both been identified as Catholic priests. After standing up to the authorities and refusing to make a plea in court, Margaret was sentenced to *"peine forte et dure"* (strong and harsh punishment).

Despite a number of twists and turns in the coming days, including several potential reprieves, Margaret was brutally executed by being crushed to death beneath heavy weights in the toll booth on Ouse Bridge on 25 March 1586. This is surely one of the darkest and saddest days in York's long history. It's also possible that Margaret's death was a critical event in the radicalisation of the young Guy Fawkes, her fellow Catholic convert in the city who was around sixteen years old at the time.

Following her martyrdom, Margaret become known as the Pearl of York. She was canonised in 1970 by Pope Paul VI as one of the Forty Catholic Martyrs of England and Wales. The next time you visit York, I'd strongly recommend a visit to the small shrine and chapel dedicated to the memory of Saint Margaret Clitherow. The chapel is located on the narrow historic Medieval street of the Shambles.

The Shambles is where the Clitherow family lived in Tudor York, although the shrine may be on the opposite side of the street from their own home, as some of the house numbers have been changed during the intervening centuries. You may also like to visit the Bar Convent on Blossom Street, where you'll find an exhibit on display of a relic jar which is said to contain one of Saint Margaret's hands.

Alternatively, if you'd like to find out more about Margaret's fascinating story, you might like to read my non-fiction history book, *"Power, Treason and Plot in Tudor England - Margaret Clitherow, an Elizabethan Saint"*. As well as exploring the personal and local intrigue behind the life and death of Margaret Clitherow, the book also examines the wider contexts of the religious power games taking place in Tudor England and the impact they had on the people of York.

Following Margaret's untimely death, the authorities were determined to apprehend Fathers Ingleby and Mush. Unfortunately for him, Father Ingleby was spotted, even though he was wearing plain clothes, near to Bishopthorpe Palace. He was suspected of being a Catholic priest due to the deference and religious gestures being made to him by another man. After being stopped, arrested and questioned, he was imprisoned and placed on trial by the Council of the North. In June 1586, Francis Ingleby was hanged, drawn and quartered at the gallows on the Knavesmire in York.

The former Member of Parliament Henry Cheke was one of many officials who'd been involved in the trials of Marmaduke Bowes, Margaret Clitherow and Francis Ingleby. At the time, Cheke was one of the officers of the Council of the North. Following Father Ingleby's death, Cheke was overheard making disparaging and insulting remarks about the dead priest.

A few hours later Henry Cheke was found dead at the bottom of a stairwell at the King's Manor. Whether this was due to a simple accident or the result of a violent act of revenge, we don't know. When his body was found, his neck was broken. He was buried afterwards in York Minster,

With Dorothy Vavasour still in prison and Margaret Clitherow now dead, the Catholic community in York needed additional people to step forward to harbour the fugitive Catholic priests who remained there. To do so, after all that had happened would be a courageous act indeed. One such person was Richard Langley. We know he provided shelter for Father Mush and for several other priests, probably including Father Ingleby before his arrest.

Langley created a series of secret chambers beneath the ground in his house in York for the priests to hide in. In October 1586, the Council of the North received a tip off. The Earl of Huntingdon and a supporting group of pursuivants and soldiers arrived at Langley's house. During their search of the building, the pursuivants discovered and apprehended two Catholic priests, Father Johnson and Father Mush. Richard Langley was also arrested. All three prisoners were taken to York Castle.

The Council of the North decided to offer Langley a deal. If he would renounce his Catholicism and inform on the other people in York who were aiding the priests, they would spare his life. Like so many of York's Catholics, Richard Langley was a brave man. He rejected the offer.

Concerned there was a chance he would be acquitted; the Council of the North replaced the members of the jury which had initially been selected to hear Langley's trial with another group of men. The replacement jury found him guilty, and he was sentenced to death. During their own trials, Father Mush and Father Johnson were also both adjudged to have committed treason and they too were condemned to death.

Awaiting their executions, Langley and the priests were separated and housed in different cells. With little time to lose, Father Mush, Father Johnson and another priest made a break for freedom. There's no record of how they did it, but all three men got away. The Earl of Huntingdon was furious. Having promised Langley's brother that Langley would not be executed before the next assizes court came to York during the spring, the Earl went back on his word. Richard Langley was hanged in York in December 1586.

Father Mush survived though. Following his time in York, he went to go on to have many more scrapes and adventures. In fact, he's the reason we know so much about the life of Margaret Clitherow. Sometime later he wrote her first biography *"A True Report of the Life and Martyrdom of Mrs Margaret Clitherow"*. While there's an obvious bias due to the priest's views and his pastoral relationship with Margaret, the book gives us an extraordinary insight into the life of an ordinary woman at this time. Usually, it's only queens or princesses' lives that have been documented, rather than the wife of a humble butcher.

Several versions of Father Mush's book still survive. One, for example, is located in the library at York Minster. During the Covid lockdown of 2020/21, the excellent team there scanned their copy of the book and kindly passed a digital version to me to assist with my research for *"Power, Treason and Plot in Tudor England"*.

Margaret's great friend and part-time midwife Dorothy Vavasour remained in the kidcote on Ouse Bridge for another year. Unfortunately, she never left there. In October 1587, Dorothy, along with two fellow prisoners Mary Hutton and Alice Oldcorne, was temporarily placed into a cold damp cell alongside the river Ouse. This was their punishment for refusing to say which of their fellow Catholics had removed the heads of several executed priests which had been placed on display in the city centre.

Due to the dreadful conditions in their cell, all three prisoners fell ill with *"gaol fever"*. One by one, the women all died. Dorothy and her husband Thomas were survived by two daughters. It must have been a terrible time for them, just as it had been for the children of Margaret Clitherow and many others.

Between the end of 1586 and the close of Queen Elizabeth's reign in 1603, there are fewer records of missionary

Catholic priests operating in York, although some were still there. One report for instance indicates that at least three other priests, Fathers Ridyall, Redshaw and Taylor, were all active in and around the city during the 1590's.

Another priest Father Anthony Page was also in the area. Father Page was arrested in 1593 after being discovered hiding beneath a pile of hay in a stable near Heworth Moor outside York. The priest may well have been living with the Thwing family at the time. They lived nearby and were well known recusants. Father Page was found guilty and executed.

By the end of the sixteenth century, the leaders of the Corporation of York were acting much more in harmony with the wishes of the Church and the Council of the North. Despite their differences, Archbishop Sandys, Dean Hutton and the Earl of Huntingdon had all played a critical and often united role in ensuring the new laws regarding religious practice were rigorously adhered to in York.

In 1588, Archbishop Sandys became ill and died. He wasn't buried in York but at Southwell Minster in Nottinghamshire. His replacement John Piers had been the Bishop of Salisbury. He was appointed to York in 1589. During the same year, Sandys' feuding rival Matthew Hutton, the Dean of York, finally became a bishop, when he was appointed to lead the diocese of Durham.

Archbishop Piers' time in York was much quieter and less colourful than that of Archbishop Sandys. After five years, Piers died at Bishopthorpe Palace in 1594. This, of course, was the official residence of the Archbishops of York and the palace which Archbishop Sandys had managed to wrestle back from the Earl of Huntingdon. Archbishop Piers was buried in York Minster. Following Piers' death, Matthew Hutton was finally given the role he'd probably always wanted, when the Queen announced that Hutton would be her new Archbishop of York.

The Earl of Huntingdon continued in his lengthy stint as the

Lord President of the Council of the North until his own death in 1594. After this, Archbishop Hutton was appointed to take on this role too. Effectively he became the most influential man in government and Church policy across the whole of the North of England, before being later replaced as the Lord President by William Cecil's son (and Robert Cecil's brother) the Baron Burghley, Thomas Cecil.

Matthew Hutton died aged seventy-seven, also in Bishopthorpe Palace, in 1606 and was buried at York Minster. If visiting the Minster today, you can see still a monument to his life and service in the south aisle of the choir.

Recusancy cases continued in York until the end of and beyond the reign of Elizabeth I. Sometimes the numbers rose and sometimes they fell. One interesting case of recusancy is linked to Henry Maye, the stepfather of Margaret Clitherow who'd been the Lord Mayor of York at the time of her trial and execution. Following Henry's own death in 1596, he was buried in the nave of the Church of St Martin's in Coney Street. He left behind his second wife Anne and their two sons Edward and Henry.

Anne Maye remarried a local man called Gabriel Thwaites. As it turns out, Thwaites was a Catholic. In 1598, he was listed as being a recusant in Henry Mayes' old parish of St Martin's in Coney Street. Thwaites must also have had some influence over his stepsons. Before long, both boys were being cited for failing to take communion and not attending the church. During the reign of James I, the younger Henry Maye was formally accused of recusancy along with his stepfather.

The Catholic recusant community in York had clearly been impacted by the execution of priests and lay people like Marmaduke Bowes and Margaret Clitherow. Nevertheless, they refused to go away.

CHAPTER THIRTY
What Next for York?

During the final two decades of the sixteenth century, many parts of England suffered from new epidemics, failed harvests and famines. Although York was at times touched by some of these, the city didn't experience anything like as major an impact as was felt elsewhere. For example, during the widespread famine of 1585 to 1587, which had spread out across much of mainland Europe and the British Isles, the West Riding of Yorkshire suffered from high death rates, but there was no major impact in York, itself.

During 1592-93, London and other parts of the country were struck down by a major outbreak of bubonic plague. Despite this, the terrible disease was prevented from entering York. Similarly, when plague affected several other parts of northern England in 1597 and 1598, it didn't get into York.

When poor harvests and resulting famines were encountered across many areas of England in 1596-98, for a time the death rates did begin to rise in some of York's poorer parishes. To ensure most of the people in the city had enough bread to eat, grain was imported from Nottinghamshire and Leicestershire and from as far away as mainland Europe. When one York merchant tried to raise the price of corn, the future bishop John King preached a sermon in York Minster in which he likened prohibitively high corn prices to the sin of usury. Archbishop Sandys would have been proud of him.

In 1601, another earthquake struck York. *The Antiquities of*

York book states *"This year in October was a great earthquake in most parts of York"*. There are few records available of what the impact was on the city, but perhaps once again parts of the population feared this was a bad omen regarding the Queen's health.

The reign of Queen Elizabeth I in general had been a positive time for many of York's people, certainly if compared to the tenures of her grandfather, father and half-siblings. Admittedly, there were notable exceptions, including many Catholics and the poorest in the city, although the second group usually didn't fare well no matter who the monarch was.

It's been estimated that the city's population is likely to have significantly recovered and increased in size during Elizabeth's reign from its low point under Edward and Mary of around eight thousand to somewhere in the region of twelve or thirteen thousand people.

By 1603, York's merchants were actively trading with many countries across the Baltic, areas of France, Spain, modern day Germany and the Low Countries. The goods being imported into York during the early 1600's had changed and expanded to include rye, flax, iron, wine, honey, olive oil, paper, figs, cooking pots, soap and many other things.

One balladeer, William Elderton, even wrote a song in which he shared his view of just how great a city York had become under Elizabeth I. A selection of the verses and the chorus of *"York, York for My Money"* are shown below. I haven't included the full lyrics, as in total there are twenty-two verses.

If you fancy having a go and singing along to the words, the ballad can be sung to the famous tune of *"Greensleeves"*. This melody is believed to have been composed around the time of Elizabeth's father Henry VIII although, in contrast to a popularly held belief, it was probably not written by him.

Verse 1:

As I came through the north country, The fashions of the world to see,

I sought for my merry company, To go to the city of London.

And when to the city of York I came, I found good company in the same,

As well disposed to every game, As if it had been at London.

Chorus:

York, York for my money, Of all the cities that ever I see,

For merry pastime and company, Except the city of London.

Although William Elderton was heaping praise on York by claiming it was the best city in England bar one, perhaps one or two people might still take issue with him for thinking London was better than York. In the second verse, Elderton tells the story of a grand archery contest which was held in York during his visit to the city.

Verse 2:

And in that city what saw I then, Knights, squires and gentlemen,

A shooting went for matches ten, As if it had been at London.

And they shot at twenty pounds a bow, Besides great cheer they did bestow;

I never saw a gallanter show, Except I had been at London.

Chorus:

York, York for my money, Of all the cities that ever I see,

For merry pastime and company, Except the city of London.

By the time Elderton gets to the tenth verse, the balladeer is so fulsome in his praise for the Lord Mayor and the Corporation's aldermen for keeping such good rule in York that he adjudges it to actually be just as good as it was in London.

Verse 10:

The Mayor of York with his company, Were all in the fields, I warrant ye

To see good rule kept orderly, As if it had been at London, Which was a dutiful sight to see, The Mayor and aldermen there to be,

For setting forth of archery As well as they do at London.

One of the later verses highlights the presence of three foreign ambassadors in York. At least one of these men hailed from Russia, perhaps all three did. Although the song was written a few decades after the visit of Envoy Nepeya, the words highlight the growing importance and influence of the city, along with the important trading links which were by now in place with Russia and other Baltic states.

Verse 13:

At York were ambassadors three, Of Russia—lords of high degree,

This shooting they desired to see, As if it had been at London;

And one desired to draw a bow, The force and strength thereof to know,

And for his delight he drew it so, As seldom seen in London.

Finally in his last verse, William Elderton makes a strong recommendation to the Queen that she should travel north to visit the city. Although the majority of the population would have been delighted to see her, probably some of York's Catholics wouldn't have been quite so keen.

Verse 22:

God grant that (once) Her Majesty, Would come, her city of York to see,

For the comfort great of that country, As well as she doth at

London.
Nothing shall be thought too dear, To see her highness'
person there,
With such obedient love and fear, As ever she had in
London.
Chorus:
York, York for my money, Of all the cities that ever I see,
For merry pastime and company, Except the city of London.

Unfortunately for the city and the people of York, the by now aging Queen declined to take up the offer. Unlike her grandfather Henry VII and her father Henry VIII, Elizabeth I didn't travel as far north as York. The closest she got was somewhere near Peterborough. Royal journeys were huge affairs in Tudor times, tiresome and expensive. It's so much easier and faster to travel north on the train these days.

After one hundred and eighteen years, the Tudor period came to an end on 24 March 1603 with the death of Queen Elizabeth I, unmarried and childless. There was now a major risk that the succession to the English throne would be contested, and the country would be thrown into a bloody civil war.

The Wars of the Roses had ended with the Tudors on the throne, but that was a distant memory. If there was to be a war, this time it would much more likely to be between Protestants and Catholics rather than rival supporters of the Houses of York and Lancaster. With its long history, close links to several rebellions and a sectarian population, York could easily have found itself once more becoming a magnet for violence and war.

In the years which preceded Elizabeth's death, the leading members of her government and the Church had recalled what had happened under the reign of Queen Mary. The Catholic Queen's bloody purge against Protestants had resulted in nearly three hundred people being executed in England and Wales in less than six years. The country's leaders must have wondered what might happen next. After all, their regime had blood on its hands too and some of the country's Catholics would be keen for revenge. During Elizabeth's time on the throne, around two hundred of the nation's Catholics had been executed for crimes relating to their faith.

In York, the numbers were quite different. Not a single religious execution of a Protestant had taken place during the reign of Queen Mary, but many Catholics had lost their lives in the city under Elizabeth. Those who'd died included priests, lay people and a woman in the form of Margaret Clitherow. They had all been executed on the orders of the state. Others too, had died while being held in York's prison cells, for example Dorothy Vavasour and her two cellmates.

Elizabeth's cousin Mary Stuart, the former Queen of Scots, was no longer a threat or a candidate for the English throne. She'd already been beheaded due to her alleged links with a Catholic plot. However, a number of other Catholics and Protestants did have valid claims.

To ensure there was to be a Protestant succession, Elizabeth's Secretary of State Robert Cecil engineered the accession of the Scots King James VI to the throne of England. James Stuart was the son of Mary Queen of Scots, although he'd been separated from his mother as an infant and raised as a Protestant. When Elizabeth I died, messages were sent to Edinburgh. James prepared to travel to Westminster to be crowned as James I, the first Stuart King of England.

In April 1603, James Stuart did something which none of his three most recent predecessors, Edward VI, Mary I and Elizabeth I, had done. During his triumphant and celebratory journey towards his coronation in London, James visited York. To ensure his arrival and stay in the city would be treated as a suitably royal occasion and celebration, James issued orders for many royal trappings to be brought north to York from London. They included items of royal clothing, grand coaches, heralds and trumpeters.

Just as they had done for Henry VII, York's authorities and people gave the soon to be King of England a warm welcome. A series of grand celebrations were held in the city. During one ceremony held at the Pavement in the centre of York (the place where the Earl of Northumberland had been beheaded after the failed Rising of the North), James was unofficially proclaimed as the new King of England.

As well as the huge crowd of local people, those recorded as being present that day included the Lord President of the Council of the North Thomas Cecil. York's Lord Mayor the haberdasher Robert Watter and the city's aldermen, sheriffs and councillors also attended. No doubt, the Archbishop of York Matthew Hutton was also present.

King James was delighted with the welcome he'd received and declared York to be England's *"second city"*, echoing the sentiments of William Elderton's ballad. Before he departed from York, the King promised to address some of the things the city's leaders had asked of him, including a request once again to dredge sections of the river Ouse to ease the import and export of goods.

When James Stuart finally left the city, he travelled to the house of Sir Edmund Stanhope in Grimston near Tadcaster, where he stayed overnight. While he was there, James knighted the Lord Mayor of York, who returned to the city as Sir Robert Watter.

Two months later, James's wife, the new Queen of England, Anne of Denmark, also stopped overnight in York on her way down from Edinburgh to London. She'd brought with her some of her children, including her older son Prince Henry and her elder daughter the Lady Elizabeth. The family and their entourage were *"nobly welcomed by the Lord Mayor and citizens"*.

Not long after this though, disaster struck the city. During the long reign of Queen Elizabeth, all plagues and epidemics had been kept outside the city walls. In 1604, pestilence returned. The great plague of that year is reported to have killed 3,512 people in York, a staggering figure of around one in four people in the city. Around this time several of the aldermen also died, probably of the plague. The men included Thomas Harrison who'd been the Lord Mayor in 1592 and Andrew True.

Over the next few years, the people of York were forced to endure a succession of severe and prolonged frosts. Two winters were so severe that the river Ouse froze over completely. Horse racing events and games of football were played on the icy surface of the water.

The religious differences which had created so much animosity between York's Protestants and Catholics during the reign of Queen Elizabeth continued. After initially promising a more tolerant approach towards England's Catholic population, King James became enraged by plots against him and changed his mind. The country's religious laws and policies hardened, impacting the people in York and elsewhere.

It was this which triggered Robert Catesby's plan to kill the King during the opening of Parliament in what we now know as the Gunpowder Plot. Most of the Catholics he gathered around him had strong connections to Tudor York.

Guy Fawkes had been born there. Jack and Kit Wright were schooled in the city. Thomas Percy was married to their sister. Thomas and Robert Wintour's uncle Father Francis Ingleby had been executed in York in 1586 for being a Catholic priest. Although ultimately they failed, in 1605 this small group of men with such strong links to York nearly brought down the whole Stuart dynasty when it had only just begun.

Day to day life in York went on as before. From time to time, there were epidemics, religious unrest and problems with the weather. In the middle of the seventeenth century, there was also the English Civil War. To examine what happened next to York in more detail, perhaps someone should write a new book about the city during the time of the Stuarts?

Meanwhile, I hope you've enjoyed reading this book about Tudor York. Perhaps you'll see the city in a different light when you next visit or, if you've not been before, you'll be inspired to come for the first time.

If you have been *informed* and/or *entertained*, perhaps you'll be kind enough to post a rating or a review on Goodreads and/or Amazon to let other potential readers know about the book. This will help raise funds for St Leonard's Hospice in York and perhaps even inspire me to continue my research and write the next one.

Thank you.

Selected Bibliography

Aveling, J. C. H., 1970. Catholic Recusancy in the City of York 1558-1791, (Catholic Record Society).

Bastow, S., 2013. Edwin Sandys, Archbishop of York 1577–88, 'Stiff-Necked, Wilful and Obstinate': Conflict in the Elizabethan Church, (Northern History, 50(2), pp.239-256).

Bede, C., 1904. Lives of the English Martyrs: Under Henry VIII, (Longmans, Green and Co.).

Bennett, M.J., 1990. Henry VII and the Northern Rising of 1489, (The English Historical Review, 105(414), pp.34-59).

Bishop, J., 2016. Currency, conversation, and control: Political discourse and the coinage in mid-Tudor England, (The English Historical Review, 131(551), pp.763-792).

Brooks, F.W., 1954. York and the Council of the North (No. 5), (Borthwick Publications).

Burrows, E., 1966, Poor relief in Tudor England, (University of Richmond Thesis).

Burton, E.H. and Pollen J.H., 1914. Lives of the English Martyrs: 1583-1588, (Longmans, Green and Co.).

Challoner, R., 1839. Memoirs of Missionary Priests and other Catholics of both sexes, that have suffered death in England on religious accounts, from the year 1577 to 1684, (John T Green).

Dickens, A.G., 1937. The marriage and character of Archbishop Holgate, (English Historical Review, Volume 52).

Dickens, A. G., 1938. The Yorkshire Submissions to Henry VIII,

1541, (English Historical Review, Volume 53).

Drake, F., 1736. Eboracum or the History and Antiquities of City of York, (London).

Ellis, I.P., 1970. The Archbishop and the Usurers, (The Journal of Ecclesiastical History, 21(1), pp.33-42).

Gee, Henry, 1898. The Elizabethan Clergy and the Settlement of Religion, 1558-1564, (Clarendon Press)

Fletcher, A. and MacCulloch, D., 2014. Tudor Rebellions: Revised 5th Edition, (Routledge).

Fraser, A., 2010. Mary Queen of Scots, (Hachette UK).

Haigh, C., 1993. English Reformations, Religion, Politics and Society Under the Tudors, (Clarendon Press).

Hildyard, C. and Torr, J., 1719. The Antiquities of York City, and the Civil Government Thereof, (Hildyard).

History of Parliament website: https://www.historyofparliamentonline.org/

Holland, N., 2017. The Real Guy Fawkes, (Pen and Sword).

Holmes, P., 1982. Resistance and Compromise, The Political Thought of the Elizabethan Catholics, (Cambridge University Press).

Hoyle, R.W. and Ramsdale, J.B., 2004. The royal progress of 1541, the north of England, and Anglo-Scottish relations, 1534–1542, (Northern History, 41(2), pp.239-265).

Johansen, Sarah, 2020. 'That silken Priest': Catholic disguise and anti-popery on the English Mission (1569–1640), (Historical Research, Volume 93)

Kesselring, K.J., 2013. Mary Queen of Scots and the Northern Rebellion of 1569, (Leadership and Elizabethan Culture, pp.51-72).

Knipe, W., 1867. Criminal Chronology of York Castle: With a

Register of Criminals Capitally Convicted and Executed at the County Assizes, Commencing March 1st, 1379, to the Present Time, (CL Burdekin).

Lake, P., and Questier, M., 2019. The Trials of Margaret Clitherow: Persecution, Martyrdom and Politics of Sanctity in Elizabethan England, (Bloomsbury).

Lewycky, N., 2009. Cardinal Thomas Wolsey and the city of York, 1514–1529, (Northern History, 46(1), pp.43-60).

Manning, R.B., 1974. Patterns of Violence in Early Tudor Enclosure Riots, (Albion, 6(2), pp.120-133).

McGovern, J., 2020. The sheriffs of York and Yorkshire in the Tudor period, (Northern History, 57(1), pp.60-76).

Morgan, T., 2022. Power, Treason and Plot in Tudor England: Margaret Clitherow, an Elizabethan Saint, (Pen and Sword).

Morris, J,, (Editor), 1872-1877. The Troubles of Our Catholic Forefathers Related by Themselves, (Burns and Oates).

Mush, J., 1619. A True Report of the Life and Martyrdom of Mrs Margaret Clitherow, (Published and transcribed several times).

Musson, R.M.W., 2008. The seismicity of the British Isles to 1600, (British Geological Survey Technical, Report OR/08/049).

Palliser, D. M., 1971, The Reformation in York 1534-1553, (Borthwick Papers No. 40, 1971).

Palliser, D.M., 1973. Epidemics in Tudor York, (Northern History, 8(1), pp.45-63).

Palliser, D. M., 1979, Tudor York, (Oxford University Press).

Palliser, D.M., 1982. Civic mentality and the environment in Tudor York, (Northern History, 18(1), pp.78-115).

Parker, M., 1853. Correspondence of Matthew Parker: comprising letters written by and to him, from AD 1535, to his death, AD 1575 (Vol. 33), (University Press).

Raithby, J., (Editor), 1811. The Statutes at Large of England and of Great Britain, Volume IV From 1553 to 1640, (G. Eyre).

Reid, R.R., 1906. The rebellion of the earls, 1569, (Transactions of the Royal Historical Society, 20, pp.171-203).

Rex, R., 2004. Vavasour, Thomas. Oxford Dictionary of National Biography.

Sandys, E., 2007. The Sermons of Edwin Sandys, DD, Successively Bishop of Worcester and London, and Archbishop of York: To Which Are Added Some Miscellaneous Pieces by the Same Author, (Wipf and Stock Publishers).

Sellers, M., 1894. The city of York in the sixteenth century, (The English Historical Review, 9(34), pp.275-304).

Speed, J. and Hawkyard, A., 1988. The counties of Britain: a Tudor atlas, (Pavilion).

Strype, J., 1821. The life & acts of Matthew Parker. 1821 (Vol. 20), (Clarendon Press).

Tillott, P.M. ed., 1961. A History of Yorkshire: The City of York (Vol. 1). (London: Published for the Institute of Historical Research by the Oxford University Press).

Toy, P., 2016. A History of St Peter's School circa 1557–1644 at the Union Terrace Site, (York Archaeological Trust).

Anon, 1850. The Fawkes's of York in the Sixteenth Century: including Notices of the Early History of Guye Fawkes, the Gunpowder Plot Conspirator, (The Athenaeum. (1195), pp.992–993).

Printed in Great Britain
by Amazon